Buffett On F.I.R.E

A Practical Guide To Achieving Your Financial Freedom Using The Buffett Way!

Benjamin Chua

Contents

Acknowledgment

I would like to thank Warren Buffett even though he did not participate in the writing of this book; however, I am always indebted to him for his wisdom and generosity over the years. In years to come, his genius as an investor will be far surpassed by his tremendous philanthropy – The Buffett foundation, which will be the world's wealthiest charitable foundation, providing for many future generations to come based on Buffett's passion for investing.

Next, I would like to thank my parents and sister for their constant love and support; my friends Ethelbert, Kevin, Samuel and Nicholas for their valuable feedback.

Lastly, I would like to dedicate this book to my wife for always being my pillar of love, support as well as F.I.R.E partner in this life journey!

May God Bless You All!

Benjamin

Disclaimer

This publication contains the opinions and ideas of its author. It is not a recommendation to purchase or sell the securities of any of the companies or investments herein discussed. It is sold with the understanding that the authors and publisher are not engaged in rendering legal, accounting, investment, or other professional services. Laws vary from state to state and federal laws may apply to a particular transaction, and if the reader requires expert financial or other assistance or legal advice, a competent professional should be consulted. Neither the authors nor the publisher can guarantee the accuracy of the information contained herein.

The authors and publisher specifically disclaim any responsibility for any liability, loss, or risk, professional or otherwise, which is incurred as a consequence, directly or indirectly, of the use and application of any of the contents of this book.

Foreword

What do I want to achieve in this life?

How can I gain financial freedom?

How can I spend more time and money on my loved ones?

Having attended countless courses and read many books, I somehow feel that there is always a gap. People didn't understand the WHY which made them pursue their financial independence and freedom. Or worse, people were just chasing after quick money. Personally, I felt a void in my life at the beginning when I was just trying to chase after fast money blindly. With the wrong mindset, I actually lost money which was entrusted to me by my loved ones. This taught me a great lesson in life.

So I embarked on my journey to learn about the various investing methodologies and strategies. The truth is that the investment world is filled with just too many strategies and knowledge.

However, I was blessed and fortunate to learn from a Buffett.

Someone once asked me what the key elements of Warren Buffett's investing philosophy are. I replied being folly or foolish as well as being disciplined and patient are key, because other people's follies will meet with Buffett's discipline and patience.

This form of investing made Buffett the 3rd richest man in the world as of 2019. Buffett is the only billionaire who made it to the Forbes list solely by investing in the stock market.

I now realize that achieving above-average return is not only a matter of which stocks you pick but also how you strategize and structure your portfolio.

To achieve a focused portfolio, you will need to acquire investing competence, patience, and a certain kind of personal temperament. This book will help you think through your WHY and how you can build a sustainable portfolio. It will give you the tools and framework to select your investment strategy ranging from index investing, dividends investing, and value investing.

Buffett is a collector of businesses; he has spent the majority of his life searching for fundamentally strong companies and businesses. Buffett wasn't just buying a stock or a share; he was buying a business. Buffett was very careful about the price he paid for a business. He was looking for a good deal. This shows two main considerations Buffett always has: What to buy based on the fundamentals and at what price to buy? In this book, we will touch on these aspects: how to identify good stocks and the price consideration.

Buffett never seemed to worry about Wall Street and the Dow Jones Industrial Average. In fact, if someone were to give Buffett a stock tip, he would have shut them off. He didn't have to rely on market sentiments or analysts' reviews.

I also began reading the old Berkshire Hathaway annual reports and Buffett's letters to his shareholders, which gave us insights into Buffett's thoughts on his investing methodologies. This was coupled with reading Benjamin Graham's book of all times, *The Intelligent Investor*. It was Graham who also influenced Buffett's business perspective of investing which forms the foundation of Buffett's investing philosophy.

As we go through the book, imagine us – you, me and Buffett – having a chat over a cup of coffee. In this book, I will share investment strategies and step-by-step ways to achieve F.I.R.E in a close-up, simple, and interactive manner.

In the first half of the book, you will learn the framework on how to identify your WHY, how to set up your personal finance model for success and how to identify your end goal with a retirement plan in mind. You will also learn the investment strategies and ideologies.

In the second half of the book, I will delve deep into the various investing methodologies mentioned by Buffett which can help you to achieve your "Financial Independence, Retire Early" (F.I.R.E) lifestyle in a sustainable model. There will be practical steps provided and explained; the idea is to really allow you to take practical steps after you have read this book.

When I was planning the content of the book, I wrote it in a manner explaining the entire process from identifying your WHY to investment strategies and even to managing your portfolio. The chapters will first introduce the concepts before going into the details which will provide you immense understanding and deep insights. The book is written to allow anyone to pick up and read it in the most comfortable manner, on the way to school, work or anywhere else.

This book will inspire you to achieve your financial freedom and time by equipping you with the investing competence to grow your happiness and wealth. Through achieving your F.I.R.E, it may also help you gain back time with your family and loved ones, and open up new opportunities to pursue your purpose and aspiration in life.

Let's go achieve your F.I.R.E the Buffett way!

Benjamin Chua

2019

Chapter 1

Understanding Your WHY

Financial freedom may mean different things to different people. Have you ever thought of having enough wealth or cash-flow to sustain your lifestyle without having to ever work again? Imagine that!

How do people do that?

One way is to work very hard to earn lots of money to have enough savings for retirement or, it may mean acquiring assets that can generate enough passive income to pay for your expenses.

Ultimately, it is important to first understand and know why you want to achieve financial freedom and how it can bring joy to your life and those around you.

For example, you need to know the WHY in your pursuit of this financial freedom.

- Freedom to do whatever you want
- Freedom to travel the world
- Freedom to spend more time with family
- Freedom to pursue your hobby and passion
- Freedom to choose your work
- Freedom to leverage opportunities

- Freedom to have the resources to give back and contribute to the world and people

If one is able to achieve financial freedom, you can pursue all the opportunities in life!

For one to pursue this journey of financial freedom, you got to:

- want this badly
- willing to be hungry enough to acquire the knowledge
- know your end goal in mind

Attaining financial freedom means you will have more assets to sustain the expenses and liabilities. When you have attained financial freedom, you have the power to determine your options in life and no longer be chained to that rat race which most will be running for the rest of their lives!

Though this is a very short chapter, you will need to spend time to pen down your WHY which will form your largest motivation and drive to attain this fulfillment.

Chapter 2

F.I.R.E

What is this "financial independence, retire early" (F.I.R.E) concept?

After understanding what financial independence will be like, there has been a new F.I.R.E concept making its way around the Internet – "Financial Independence, Retire Early". This is a movement which requires huge discipline that allows one to retire early! You will need to commit a high saving rate, e.g. 70%, to build up a huge investment fund and thereafter, you will be able to quit your job in your 40s or 50s while living off the investment funds.

Once you have accumulated the investment fund required based on your retirement goals (recommended about 30 times your yearly expenses as a ballpark figure), you can quit your job. Next, you can draw down on your investment funds, averaging about 3 to 4% per year. This draw-down model is recommended though you need to watch the expenses to ensure the investment funds can be sustainable. Should you require more coverage and have a higher retirement goal, it is good to go for the passive income route than the draw-down model.

After achieving F.I.RE, does it mean I got to quit my job?

When you have achieved the F.I.R.E, it doesn't mean you have to quit your day job. It all goes back to the end goal and life's purpose. It is about retiring early and having the freedom to pursue your own dreams and ambitions passionately. Supposed your day job is something that you are really passionate about and derives you much joy and happiness in a purposeful way, having achieved F.I.R.E will allow you more time, peace of mind and resources to pursue your passion more fervently.

In fact, you should ask yourself what is the real purpose of achieving F.I.R.E.

If you are dying to retire early because you don't like your job then it probably may be a bad reason to do so. Once you quit your job, you may end up finding yourself being bored or wandering around aimless. Early retirement is less for people who hate their jobs and more for those who have a clear idea of a different lifestyle or goal they may want to pursue.

Remember that achieving FIRE is just one of the mediums to achieve the end goal and should not be the end goal itself.

It is also good to know that it takes a lot of effort and determination to achieve F.I.R.E and the underlying motivation and purpose have to be very strong for one to have such conviction. Sometimes, it might mean cutting back on expenses or having to earn an above average income. For some, the drive to increase income will be strong to close the gap. Ultimately, it is how we can incorporate the F.I.R.E principles as part of our lives which will go the distance to create sustainable wealth!

Well, studies have shown that out of 100 people who start work at age 25, by the time they reach age 65;

- 1% will be considered wealthy (financial freedom on their terms)

- 3% will have adequate savings to be secured without any financial help
- 7% will still be working...because they have to (not because they want to)
- 74% are dependent on the Age Pension, family, friends or charity
- the other 15%? ...well, unfortunately, they don't make it to age 65

Why some people can achieve F.I.R.E? How do you incorporate it as a lifestyle?

They set it as their life goal to attain financial freedom and F.I.R.E.

They save more than they spend, usually saving up to 70% of their income.

They pay themselves first.

They try to take on as little debt as possible unless it is a good debt.

They build up an emergency fund, usually 6 to 12 months of income.

They grow and protect their wealth through appropriate investment vehicles adopted by the wealthiest people.

They ensure and protect themselves adequately in the event of income loss, accidents, health problems, illnesses, death, etc.

They start saving, investing and compounding their wealth as early as they can.

They do their due diligence, risk management and make sound financial decisions.

They do not accept the status quo and are hungry enough to make a difference.

They know their retirement, investment, and life goals – they track their performance.

They have a life plan, and have the discipline to stick to it!

Regardless of your background, phase in life, knowing how to invest and achieving F.I.R.E is important and useful for anyone who wants to live his/her dreams and aspiration in life. Ultimately, you want to beat the rat race and this game of life which we all get to play it once!

Chapter 3

How To Be Like Mr. Buffett

(My Inspiration!)

In order to achieve F.I.R.E and investing competency, the next question is who can be this beacon or model for us to follow? It is always best to follow the path of someone, in this case in the investment world, who can guide and inspire us to reach the same financial literacy and wealth status we hope to achieve through investing.

Who can be this beacon of light?

My personal idol is Warren Buffett who is famous for being one of the most successful investors of all time.

Buffett's success is astounding considering his life's work has been almost in investing. He has a very remarkable ability to identify right investments at the right time making him a titan in the investing world. Currently, his net worth is about $85billions, which places him among the top 3 richest people in the world! Can you imagine that?

By the way, he also owns the Berkshire Hathaway company.

Quick Highlights

- Buffett was born in 1930 in Omaha, Nebraska.
- He was picking out stocks at 11 years old and had amassed the equivalent of US$53,000 in today's dollars by the time he was 16.
- He instead went to Columbia University's business school and finished with a Master's degree in economics. Buffett was hardly settling: His hero, economist, and author of *The Intelligent Investor,* Benjamin Graham, taught at the school.
- One of Buffett's main tenets of investing in business was to pick companies in stable industries. The other one was to simply pick companies whose products he enjoyed.
- He started investing in Coke in 1988 and soon owned 7% of the company, worth over US$1 billion.
- His net worth comes from his various shares and his portfolio. His yearly salary is US$100,000.
- It wasn't until 1985, 20 years after his takeover of Berkshire Hathaway, that his various investments and businesses gave him a net worth of US$1 billion. He was 55 years old.
- Buffett still owns the house he purchased in Omaha back in 1958. The house, with 5 bedrooms and 2.5 bathrooms, was purchased for US$31,500. In today's dollars, that is the equivalent of over US$274,000.
- In 2006, he made a pledge to eventually give all of his Berkshire Hathaway shares to philanthropic causes and foundations.
- One of his more-recent donations came in 2017 when he converted some of his Class B shares of Berkshire Hathaway into US$3.4 billion. That money was

divided into 5 sums that went to the Bill & Melinda Gates Foundation, his own foundation (the Susan Thomas Buffett foundation, named after his late first wife) and 3 charities each run by his children.

- He is 89 years old as of 2019.
- Warren Buffett, the chairman, and CEO of Berkshire Hathaway has a net worth of about US$85 billion.
- Buffett is a generous philanthropist having given away more than $27 billion in the last decade.
- The billionaire is known for his frugal habits, like his daily McDonald's breakfast and insistence on using a flip phone.
- His modest home in Nebraska is worth just 0.001% of his total wealth and he never spends more than US$3.17 on his daily McDonald's breakfast.
- The longevity of Buffett's outperformance is greater than that of other savvy investors, such as David Einhorn and Walter Schloss.
- US$1,000 invested in Buffett's Berkshire Hathaway stock back in 1964, when Buffett took over the company and shares cost just US$19, would be worth about US$13 million dollars today.
- Buffett's net worth is greater than the GDP of Uruguay.
- He doesn't think money equals success: 'I measure success by how many people love me. And the best way to be loved is to be lovable.'

Most people recognize Warren Buffett as the most successful exponent of value investing. And with good reason too – Buffett is currently the third richest man in the world and his holding company, Berkshire Hathaway, has seen its per-share book value grow from US$19 in 1964 to US$211,750 in 2017, a rate of 19.1% compounded annually over 53 years.

Between 1957 and 1969, Buffett had generated an annualized return of 29.5% applying the methods taught by Graham. These were Buffett's *highest* returns over his career:

"The highest rates of return I've ever achieved were in the 1950s. I killed the Dow. You ought to see the numbers. I think I could make you 50% a year on $1 million. No, I know I could. I guarantee that."
Warren Buffett

How to be like Warren Buffett?

Overall, Buffett's investment style can be boring and he only advocates investing in businesses which have a simple business model and one that he can understand easily. It should be within the circle of competence. He tends to keep a sizable amount of cash spare in the case to be invested into fundamentally strong companies for a very long time. In short, Warren Buffett is a strong believer of the value investing philosophy.

Value investing involves being able to assess and select companies that have high intrinsic value justified by their financial solidity, assets, earnings, and dividends. This allows investors weather through market cycles in economic pessimism and over-excitability.

Buffett believes when the prices of such fundamentally strong companies' stocks are low in proportion to their intrinsic values, smart investors should consider purchasing them. He also emphasizes the importance of looking for companies with a competitive advantage over their competitors.

However, he can also be very brutal when it comes to underperforming stocks and if he believes they are no longer worth buying, he will be quick to sell.

Overall, Buffett doesn't time the market nor does he try to predict the market. Who can really foresee the future? Instead, Buffett is prepared to invest in stocks that he is willing to buy entirely or hold for a very long time, in his own words, which is forever! The holding strategy is remarkably simple and following it could help to improve an investor's portfolio performance in the long run.

Key Strategies by Buffett

- **Think of stocks as businesses**

It is to think of stocks as owning a business. Buffett believes stockholders should see themselves as business owners in which they are investing. This helps investors like you, to focus and think more about the longer term. Furthermore, long term investors will analyze the business in greater detail, which tends to lead to improved investment returns.

- **Increase the size of your investment**

Buffett contends that over-diversification can hamper returns as much as a lack of diversification. That's why he doesn't invest in mutual funds. It's also why he prefers to make significant investments in just a handful of companies.

Buffett is a firm believer that investors have to do their homework before investing into any stock, and after the due diligence is done, the investors should feel comfortable enough to dedicate a sizable portion of the assets into that stock. They should also feel comfortable in having their overall portfolio into a handful of good companies with excellent growth prospects.

By taking time to allocate the funds properly in a focused manner, it reflects how the investor feels about the business – if the best business you own presents the least financial risk with the strongest fundamentals, why would you put money into your 20th business instead of adding money to the top choices?

- **Reduce portfolio turnover**

Buying and selling the stocks too frequent can actually hamper the investors' returns as the portfolio turnover increases the amount of transaction and commission fees. By trading too often, the investor can run the risk of investing with emotions due to the short term market fluctuations. Instead, the investors should think long term and reap the rewards of increased earnings and/or dividends over time.

- **Develop alternative benchmarks**

While the stock price can be the final indicator of the success or failure of a given investment choice, Buffett does not just focus on this metric. Instead, he focuses on the fundamentals of the businesses and if the company shows signs of growing itself profitably, the Buffett believes the share price will ultimately take care of itself. If the fundamentals are solid and the company is improving shareholder value by generating consistent bottom-line growth, the share price should reflect that in the long term.

- **Recognizing the psychological aspects of investing**

More often than not, investors' own emotions can be their worst enemy. Buffett mentioned that the key to overcoming emotions is being able to retain your belief in the real fundamentals of the business, and not get too concerned about the stock market. This means we have to understand that there is a certain psychological mindset that the successful investor tends to have. The successful investor will focus on probabilities and economic issues while letting decisions be ruled by rational, as opposed to emotional thinking.

- **Ignore market forecasts**

Buffett suggests that investors should focus their efforts on investing in shares that are not currently being accurately valued by the market. The logic here is that as the stock market begins to realize the company's intrinsic value, the investor will stand to make a lot of money. There is an old saying that the Dow climbs a wall of worry - in spite of the negativity in the marketplace, and those who keep talking about the great recession being around the corner, the markets tend to fare well over time. On the flip side, over-optimistic people will keep arguing that the stock market is headed perpetually higher. Both groups of people should be ignored in general.

Buffett's secret rules of investing

"Rule number 1 is never to lose money. Rule number 2- never forget rule number one."

Warren Buffett

Buffett is not a day trader or even a highly frequent trader but he rather focuses on buying companies which he can hold onto for the long term. In fact, one of Warren Buffett's most famous quotes is, "Our favorite holding period is forever."

Buffett advised that if you aren't comfortable holding onto a company for at least 10 years then you should never buy it. Using these simple investing principles, Warren Buffett has been able to single out companies that deliver value over the long term and buys them at a price point which has a good safety margins to their true worth.

Warren Buffett may be a legend among investors, but there is no magical secret behind his success. With this simple rule number 1 in investing, it is a grounded strategy and philosophy to help investors be prudent and extra careful when it comes to investing their money. This was the same strategy which Buffett has adopted over the course of his career till today.

With that said, by following the strategy of rule number 1 in investing, you can emulate the past success of Warren Buffett and Berkshire Hathaway in your own investments.

If You Invested US$1,000 Dollars in Berkshire Hathaway in 1964...

So, what would US$1,000 invested in Berkshire Hathaway (BRK-A) in 1964 be worth today?

Buffett first took over the holding company Berkshire Hathaway in 1964. At the time, shares of Berkshire Hathaway were valued at just US$19 a share. With Buffett at the helm choosing which companies Berkshire Hathaway invested in, though, this number rose dramatically.

Today, class A shares of Berkshire Hathaway are valued at a little over US$300,000 a share.

This means that US$1,000 invested in Berkshire Hathaway back when Buffett took over in 1964 would be worth almost US$16,000,000 today. If you had invested US*$1,000 a year* in Berkshire Hathaway starting in 1964, your returns would be even more staggering.

Today, US$1,000 a year invested in Berkshire Hathaway from 1964 to now – a total investment of US$54,000 – would be worth US*$124,000,000*.

Many of today's investors either weren't alive in 1964 when Berkshire Hathaway was taken over by Buffett. Thanks to Buffett's investment strategy, though, none of those matters – even new or current investors like you can follow the Buffett way of investing to grow your wealth.

Tips to be like Warren Buffett:

- Having along time horizon when it comes to investing. When he buys a stock, it is to hold forever.
- To invest without emotions – A famous quote by Buffett, "To be fearful when others are greedy and greedy when others are fearful." This is by far one of Buffett's most impressive skills to be able to frequently buy low and sell high.
- Always invest within your circle of confidence or competence and giving all your investments a margin of safety. The circle of competence suggests investors should stick to businesses and industries which they understand well. Having a margin of safety would mean for investors to buy a stock if it is selling for a material discount to the fair price.
- One of the most important financial ratios that you can use to gauge business quality is a return on invested capital. Companies that earn high returns on the capital tied up in their business have the potential to compound their earnings faster than lower-returning businesses. As a result, the intrinsic value of these enterprises rises over time.
- High returns on invested capital create value and are often indicative of an economic moat. You can aim to invest in companies that generate high (10 to 20% upwards) and stable returns on invested capital. Instead of giving in to the temptation to buy a dividend stock yielding 10% or snap up shares of a company trading for "just" 8x earnings, be sure you are comfortable with company's business quality.
- Buffett clearly embraces a buy-and-hold mentality. He has held some of his positions for a number of decades.

Why? For one thing, it's hard to find excellent businesses that continue to have a bright long-term future (Buffett runs a concentrated portfolio for this reason). Furthermore, quality businesses earn high returns and increase in value over time. Just like Buffett said, time is the friend of the wonderful business. Fundamentals can take years to impact a stock's price, and only patient investors are rewarded.

- Trading activity is the enemy of investment returns. Constantly buying and selling stocks eats away the returns in the form of taxes and trading commissions. Instead, we are generally better off to "buy right and sit tight."

- Some investors excessively diversify their portfolios out of fear and/or ignorance. Owning 100 stocks makes it virtually impossible for an investor to keep tabs on current events impacting their companies. Excessive diversification also means that a portfolio is likely invested in a number of mediocre businesses, diluting the impact from its high-quality holdings.

- As investors, we need to ask ourselves if a news item truly impacts our company's long-term earnings power. If the answer is no, we should probably do the opposite of whatever the market is doing (e.g. Coke falls by 4% on a disappointing earnings report caused by temporary factors – consider buying the stock).

- The stock market is an unpredictable, dynamic force. We need to be very selective with the news we choose to listen to, much less act on. In my opinion, this is one of the most important pieces of investment advice.

- It doesn't take a genius to follow Buffett's investment philosophy, but it is remarkably difficult for anyone to consistently beat the market and sidestep behavioral mistakes. Equally important, investors must remain aware that there is no such thing as a magical set of rules, a formula, or an "Easy Button" that can generate market-beating results. It doesn't exist and never will.

- Stock prices will swing with investor emotions, but that doesn't mean a company's future stream of cash flow has changed. While there is always some debate surrounding a company's future earnings stream, the margin of disagreement is usually far lower than the stock's price volatility. Investors need to distinguish between price and value, concentrating their efforts on high-quality companies trading at the most reasonable prices today.

- Investing in the stock market is not a path to get rich quickly. Investing is not meant to be exciting, and dividend growth investing, in particular, is a conservative strategy. Rather than try to find the next major winner in an emerging industry, it is often better to invest in companies that have already proven their worth.

- Buffett is obviously far more connected than any of us, which certainly helps him learn who the best and most trustworthy management teams are in a particular industry. While we lack the resources to really evaluate the character and skill of a public company's CEO for investing purposes, we can certainly control who we listen to when it comes to selecting our investments and managing our portfolios. The financial world is filled with many characters – both good and bad. Unfortunately, a number of folks realizes they can prey on investors' unrealistic expectations and feelings of fear and greed to make a quick buck.

Quotes by Warren Buffett

"And if they insist on trying to time their participation in equities, they should try to be fearful when others are greedy and greedy only when others are fearful." – 2004 Annual Shareholder Letter

"Rule No. 1: Never lose money. Rule No. 2: Never forget rule No.1."

"If you're in the luckiest 1% of humanity, you owe it to the rest of humanity to think about the other 99%."

"It's far better to buy a wonderful company at a fair price than a fair company at a wonderful price."

"If you aren't thinking about owning a stock for ten years, don't even think about owning it for ten minutes."
"Our favorite holding period is forever."

"The stock market is designed to transfer money from the active to the patient."

"Only when the tide goes out to do you discover who's been swimming naked."

"Price is what you pay. Value is what you get."

"Someone is sitting in the shade today because someone planted a tree a long time ago."

"It takes 20 years to build a reputation and five minutes to ruin it. If you think about that, you'll do things differently."

"Risk comes from not knowing what you're doing."

"It's better to hang out with people better than you. Pick out associates whose behavior is better than yours and you'll drift in that direction."

"I never attempt to make money on the stock market. I buy on the assumption that they could close the market the next day and not reopen it for five years."

"We simply attempt to be fearful when others are greedy and to be greedy only when others are fearful."

"Should you find yourself in a chronically leaking boat, energy devoted to changing vessels is likely to be more productive than energy devoted to patching leaks."

"We have learned to turn out lots of goods and services, but we haven't learned as well how to have everybody share in the bounty. The obligation of a society as prosperous as ours is to figure out how nobody gets left too far behind."

On trading out of a bad investment: *"That may seem easy to do when one looks through an always-clean, rear-view mirror. Unfortunately, however, it's the windshield through which investors must peer, and that glass is invariably fogged."*

"You only have to do a very few things right in your life so long as you don't do too many things wrong."

"Time is the friend of the wonderful business, the enemy of the mediocre."

"Opportunities come infrequently. When it rains gold, put out the buck, not the thimble."

"Diversification is a protection against ignorance. It makes very little sense for those who know what they're doing."

"You will notice that our major equity holdings are relatively few. We select such investments on a long-term basis, weighing the same factors as would be involved in the purchase of 100% of an operating business: (1) favorable long-term economic characteristics; (2) competent and honest management; (3) purchase price attractive when measured against the yardstick of value to a private owner; and (4) an industry with which we are familiar and whose long-term business characteristics we feel competent to judge. It is difficult to find investments meeting such a test, and that is one reason for our concentration of holdings. We simply can't find one hundred different securities that conform to our investment requirements. However, we feel quite comfortable concentrating our holdings in the much smaller number that we do identify as attractive."

"Owners of stocks, however, too often let the capricious and often irrational behaviors of their fellow owners cause them to behave irrationally as well. Because there is so much chatter about markets, the economy, interest rates, price behavior of stocks, etc., some investors believe it is important to listen to pundits – and, worse yet, important to consider acting upon their comments."

"Investors should be skeptical of history-based models. Constructed by a nerdy-sounding priesthood...these models tend to look impressive. Too often, though, investors forget to

examine the assumptions behind the models. Beware of geeks bearing formulas."

"Once management shows itself insensitive to the interests of owners, shareholders will suffer a long time from the price/value ratio afforded their stock (relative to other stocks), no matter what assurances management gives that the value-diluting action taken was a one-of-a-kind event."

"Wall Street is the only place that people ride to in a Rolls Royce to get advice from those who take the subway."

Warren's words of wisdom are in such demand that there have been many compiled books with his quotes and his Annual Shareholder Letters. For people trying to get an insight into how the Oracle of Omaha thinks, reading his quotes is a great way to start!

Chapter 4

How To Get Started And Getting The Foundation Right

Before we get to investing, it is critical to set the foundation right and solid. There are many ways to kick-start a good financial planning strategy for yourself. There is no right or wrong way because it really depends on what you want to achieve at the end of the day.

The reason is a lot of people will jump right into investing without getting their foundation and basic right, and end up not investing well. It is critical to get this part right because it helps you to have a disciplined mindset and strengthened will power. Plus, once you have laid the foundation in getting your personal finance right, this will create more safety layers to give you the confidence to invest and grow your investment fund!

A quick summary of some basic things for you to get your personal finance in check before we will embark on this investment journey:

1. Assess how much retirement fund is required.
2. Track your expenses, yes down to every expense spent per day.
3. Set aside 12 months' worth of expenses as part of your emergency fund. This is to help you get by should there be an urgent need for you to activate those funds.

4. Get sufficient term insurance coverage for personal accident, disability, critical illness and hospitalization (which are the basic).

5. Make plans for short term goals, for example, wedding, honeymoon, home mortgage, etc.

It is important to work out a plan and understand the financial objectives so that it gives us clarity to create a clear strategy to achieve those goals. Remember goal setting is part of the overall financial planning process!

Chapter 5

Setting Retirement Goals: How Much Do You Need?

In life, if you haven't set any financial goals for yourself, there's no way you will know it when you have hit homerun and you will be just working after money endlessly. With a financial goal in mind, this will make you more focused and determined to achieve it.

The more quantifiable and specific your financial goals, the easier it is to act upon those goals because you have clarity on them.

- I want to achieve US$100,000 by age 30.
- I want to have a US$300,000 investment portfolio by age 35.
- I want to have at least US$400,000 net-worth by age 30.
- I want to have a retirement fund at US$2.87 million to generate a passive income of US$3,000 based on a dividend yield of 5% by age 65.

There are generally two ways to assess the type of retirement funds required. One is the drawdown method which you can amass the fund and then redraw out the annual amount required for the year. The second method is to amass the fund large enough that it can pay out a passive income sufficiently for the year's expenses.

For the first method, a broad rule of thumb is to multiply your current annual spending by 25. This should be the size of your portfolio by retirement age in order for you to withdraw about 4% of that portfolio to live comfortably.

For example, if you currently spend US$40,000 per year, you will need about 25 times that amount orUS$1 million at the beginning of your retirement. This will be sufficient so that you can withdraw 4% of US$1 million in your first year of retirement. You can continue to withdraw 4% of your remaining portfolio every year, and still maintain a reasonable chance that you won't outlive your money.

Another way is to estimate your annual expenses and then to calculate your entire retirement fund based on a dividend yield of about 5%. Assuming an average inflation rate of 4%, you will need to factor your retirement fund based on a future value when you are 65 years old (typical retirement age).

E.g. you may need US$3,000 per month for expenses, plus another US$10,000 for holidays in a year. Based on this, you will require about US$46,000 in passive income. With a dividend yield of 5%, the investment fund required will be about US$920,000. However, we still need to factor in an inflation rate of 4% over the next 30 years (assuming you are 30 years old now) using a future value calculator, and your investment or retirement fund will be US$2,983,925.71.

Wealth Accumulation after 25 Years, Inflation-Adjusted

Monthly Investment	\	Annual Rate of Return										
		4%	5%	6%	7%	8%	9%	10%	11%	12%	13%	14%
	$ 3,500.00	$1.23M	$1.39M	$1.58M	$1.80M	$2.06M	$2.36M	$2.71M	$3.13M	$3.61M	$4.18M	$4.85M
	$ 3,250.00	$1.14M	$1.29M	$1.46M	$1.67M	$1.91M	$2.19M	$2.52M	$2.90M	$3.35M	$3.88M	$4.50M
	$ 3,000.00	$1.05M	$1.19M	$1.35M	$1.54M	$1.76M	$2.02M	$2.33M	$2.68M	$3.09M	$3.58M	$4.16M
	$ 2,750.00	$963k	$1.09M	$1.24M	$1.41M	$1.62M	$1.85M	$2.13M	$2.46M	$2.84M	$3.28M	$3.80M
	$ 2,500.00	$876k	$992k	$1.13M	$1.29M	$1.47M	$1.69M	$1.94M	$2.23M	$2.58M	$2.97M	$3.46M
	$ 2,250.00	$788k	$893k	$1.01M	$1.16M	$1.32M	$1.52M	$1.74M	$2.01M	$2.32M	$2.69M	$3.12M
	$ 2,000.00	$701k	$793k	$902k	$1.03M	$1.17M	$1.35M	$1.55M	$1.79M	$2.06M	$2.39M	$2.77M
	$ 1,750.00	$613k	$694k	$789k	$899k	$1.03M	$1.18M	$1.36M	$1.56M	$1.80M	$2.09M	$2.42M
	$ 1,500.00	$525k	$595k	$676k	$771k	$882k	$1.01M	$1.16M	$1.34M	$1.55M	$1.79M	$2.08M
	$ 1,250.00	$438k	$496k	$564k	$642k	$735k	$843k	$969k	$1.12M	$1.29M	$1.49M	$1.73M
	$ 1,000.00	$350k	$397k	$451k	$514k	$588k	$674k	$775k	$895k	$1.03M	$1.19M	$1.38M
	$ 750.00	$263k	$298k	$338k	$385k	$441k	$506k	$581k	$670k	$774k	$896k	$1.04M
	$ 500.00	$175k	$198k	$225k	$257k	$294k	$337k	$388k	$447k	$516k	$597k	$693k
	$ 250.00	$88k	$99k	$113k	$128k	$147k	$169k	$194k	$223k	$258k	$299k	$346k

Based on the retirement fund required, you will need to save about US$2,000 per month invested at a rate of return of 14% and above to meet your retirement goals.

There are two important things to note when it comes to achieving your retirement goals faster – you can either increase the income, or you can increase the rate of return on your investment.

Years To Reach One Million Dollars

Monthly Savings	2%	4%	6%	8%	10%	12%	14%	16%
$50	177	105	77	61	51	44	39	35
$100	144	88	66	53	44	39	34	31
$150	125	79	59	48	40	35	31	28
$200	112	72	54	44	38	33	29	26
$250	102	67	51	42	35	31	28	25
$300	94	62	48	39	34	30	26	24
$400	82	56	43	36	31	27	24	22
$500	73	51	40	33	29	25	23	21
$750	58	42	34	29	25	22	20	18
$1,000	49	37	30	25	22	20	18	17
$1,250	42	32	27	23	20	18	17	15
$1,500	37	29	24	21	19	17	16	14
$2,000	30	25	21	18	16	15	14	13
$2,500	26	21	18	16	15	13	12	12
$3,000	22	19	16	15	13	12	11	11
$4,000	17	15	14	12	11	10	10	9
$5,000	14	13	12	11	10	9	9	8

In this table, it shows the number of years it takes to reach $1 million based on the monthly saving amount and rate of return on your investment.

Chapter 6

How To Save And Improve Saving Rate

One of the most powerful tools in this world is the power of compounding! With the power of compounded interest over time, people who started investing at an early age, e.g. in their 20s, are in a very good position to grow and accumulate massive wealth by the time they retire. The truth is that many of them do not do it early enough.

If you start early, your investments can compound over a longer time period and they can generate greater returns for you.

Always remember the rule of 72.

When you divide 72 by the rate of return, this is the number of years required to double your money. So if your rate of return is 4% per annum, it will take you about 18 years to double your money with a 4% interest rate.

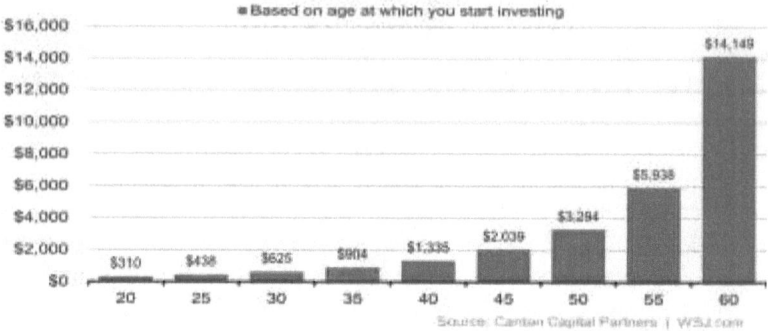

Monthly Savings Needed to Achieve $1M at Retirement
Hypothetical assumes 6.5% annual return and doesn't account for fees or taxes.

In the table above, it actually shows that you do not need to put in as much funds if you save and accumulate your wealth at an early age and this is the power of compounding. This is wonderful news for those with a lower capital to begin investing.

And for those who can maintain a good income flow for investing, it actually means you will be able to achieve a higher amount of investment funds as you approach your retirement age in 25 to 30 years' time.

Having a budget

In order to save money for investment, it is key to have a monthly budget. Personally, I do track my expenses on a daily basis using a spreadsheet. This will take into account all the income, spending expenses and investment – you need to track and write it down somewhere and somehow. The moment you lose sight of your expense tracking, it becomes difficult to keep up with your budget.

This is also a useful aspect of financial planning. Once you have kick-started this tracking of your spending, you will be able to notice some patterns in your spending habits, for example, on entertainment, coffee or shopping, etc. You will then be able to identify what you need to cut down based on your spending habits. Your saving patterns will allow you to draw up plans for short-term and long-term financial goals, such as a vacation, a new house or even F.I.R.E!

Aim to save up to 50% first, and then slowly increase the saving rate.

Your savings rate is one of the most important metrics when it comes to achieving your retirement goals. Being able to put away a large proportion of your income – especially if you're still young – will help you generate greater investment returns by the time you want to retire.

Here's what you can do to increase your savings rate:

- Cut spending. One of the ways you can increase your savings rate is, unsurprisingly, to save more. Optimizing big-ticket spending, such as housing (consider refinancing your home loan to potentially save thousands of dollars in interest charges), food (eat out less) or transportation (ditch the car) can greatly boost your savings rate.

- Save on existing spending. Using cash-back tools, discounts and coupons can help you to save further – this means saving more without having to reduce spending.
- Increase earnings. Boosting your income could mean becoming more valuable at work to negotiate a raise or a promotion, or picking up a side job for additional income. However, as your income increases, you should try to keep your increase in spending (if any) to a minimum in order to maximize your savings rate.

Chapter 7

Setting Aside Emergency Funds

An emergency fund is a sum of money set aside for any sudden life events, accidents, injuries, or even an unexpected loss of income. Essentially, it is about setting aside funds for rainy days.

Why have an emergency fund?

Having an emergency fund gives you the buffer to pay those sudden expenses so that you don't have to turn to short-term loans or worse still, credit cards to cover the lack of cash. An emergency fund should be a financial priority and should come before saving or investing for retirement.

Before we break down exactly what an emergency fund is, let's define what it is not:

- It is not used for any planned purchases like a house, a new car, a holiday, etc.
- It does not have to be a large, unattainable amount – it can start small.
- It is not a set amount for everyone – it varies based on your lifestyle and expenses.

Overall, you should put aside 8 to 12 months' worth of expenses or salary as an emergency fund. In the event of an emergency, you can take a hiatus from work without having to worry about expenses. You will have a peace of mind to handle these situations.

Having an emergency fund gives you the assurance that should something truly awful happens, such as losing your job, you can worry about how to deal with the emergency itself and not worry about how you're going to survive financially.

Chapter 8

Insurance: What To Buy?

Most people know that they need to buy insurance but sometimes, they end up paying too much premiums for them.

Insurance coverage for death, total permanent disability, and critical illness, as well as hospitalization, will be the key essentials. You will be surprised that most people do not have adequate coverage as they are already paying so much premiums for life or whole life policies for example. Worse still, they might have bought insurance-linked policies where the bulk of their premiums (close to 80% in their first and second year depending on the cost structure) are used to fund the commissions and investment instead of the actual insurance coverage itself. Adequate insurance coverage should and can be affordable.

First, we need to understand that the basis of insurance is for protection, and not for investment. Yes, we need to be very clear about this – never to lump insurance and investment together. They have to be dealt with separately.

When we purchase certain insurances, we will need to address the health risk that may cause monetary loss or challenges for ourselves and our loved ones.

The 3 common health risk areas are:

- Death or Total Permanent Disability (TPD) risk: If anything happens to you, your loved ones will have difficulties getting along with their lives with the outstanding bills and debts – get insurance for death and TPD.
- Critical illness risk: If you suffer from an advanced stage of critical illness and require expensive medical treatment but cannot afford them, this is when an insurance plan for critical illness is useful.
- Hospitalization risk: If you injure yourself and require some outpatient treatment, this will come in handy – get the hospitalization plan or integrated shield plans (some comes with additional riders).

Why buy term insurance?

Generally, there are a few types of insurance plans you can find on the market. Typically, there are term life insurance or whole life insurance. For term life insurance, it is the cheaper of the two and will protect you as you pay. There is no cash payout at maturity or anything.

For whole life insurance, it tends to be costlier in terms of premiums. There will be a cash value payout on maturity or when you choose to cancel the plan eventually. Under the family of whole life insurance, there are sub-types such as endowment plans, retirement plans or investment-linked plans which are sort of an investment plan with an insurance feature built into it.

When should you take up Term Life plan?

- You are confident that you are able to earn a higher return than the bonuses that the insurer offers you. You know the whole debate surrounding *#buyterminvesttherest*...
- You require additional coverage due to an increase in income.
- You require additional short-term coverage due to a sudden increase in liabilities (e.g. mortgage, car loans).

One of the greatest advantages in choosing term insurance over a whole life plan is the substantial savings you get to enjoy from the lower premiums paid over a lifetime. This is good for people who need insurance protection coverage at the lowest cost possible.

Let's compare the insurance premiums a person will have to pay for term and whole life insurance based on a 35 year-old man, nonsmoker with a sum assured of S$500,000. It will cost him, on average, S$15,300 compared to S$291,103 of premiums paid over a 30-year period.

Type	Life insurance policy	Annual cost	Total amount paid
Term	FWD Insurance Term Life	$510	$510 x 30 years = $15,300
Term	Great Eastern Max Term Value	$840	$510 x 30 years = $25,200
Whole life	NTUC Limited Pay Protection	$10,038	$10,038 x 29 years = $291,103
Whole life	AXA Life MultiProtect	$13,440	$13,440 x 30 years = $403,200

Can you imagine if you had used the money saved on premiums to invest? In fact, "Buy Term and Invest the rest" is a strategy which allows you to grow your money if you make the right investment decisions. One important consideration when choosing to take up a term plan is that the coverage term may expire at a time where you'll continue to need protection (or need it most).

What amount of coverage to get for each term plan?

As a rule of thumb, for:

- Death or TPD insurance coverage, it should be about 8 to10 times your annual income.
- Critical illness insurance coverage, it should be about 4 to 6 times your annual income.

Chapter 9

Short-Term Goals

Before jumping into the stock market, it is good to write down an account of your short-term goals. Some examples can be to clear your debts, tuition loan, or even to save for wedding, car, home renovation, down-payment for a house. Of course, these goals will vary depending on the life stage you are at. It is important for you to note these short-term goals down so that you can set aside the necessary funds and not use them for investing. Remember that you should not invest money which you cannot afford to lose, i.e. your wedding fund, home loan, etc.

On a piece of paper, you can write down:

- What are your short-term goals?
- When do you want to achieve them (time frame)?
- Is there any cost impact or funds required?
- What does it mean for me to save up for the fund(s)? E.g. Do I need to reduce my expenses? Or increase my income?

Here are some simple steps to save up for the short-term goals:

- Have a plan – identify your goals and the associated expenses and write them all down.
- Break things down – identify your time horizon and needs and start paying yourself first.

- Set up an auto saving account – this will continue to make a regular automatic saving contribution to your saving account.

Chapter 10

Once All The Foundation Is Taken Care Of

After finally settling the foundation of your personal finance, we are now ready to begin the investment journey!

By now, you may have read about various types of investment strategies – e.g. dividend investing, index investing, value investing, growth investing etc.

Which investment strategy should you choose from?

More zealous investors may have mentioned that the decision on the investing strategy to acquire is very clear and it will surely be aligned to Warren Buffett's strategy. However, it may not be so simple. It is also about choosing an investment strategy which you are comfortable with and can handle it emotionally and psychologically. This is a key success factor to investing well!

Hence, it is pointless to ask which investment strategy is the best because there is no holy grail of investing. The point is that any of those strategies can provide you good or even great returns, but only if you do it right!

Hence, the main question to ask is: Which investment strategy works best for me based on my risk appetite, investing character, competence and objective? It is about knowing your personal character and emotions, financial and retirement objectives, investment goals, time horizon, etc.

There are a few key considerations for you to think about:

- **How much time do you have to invest?**

When investing, the longer your time horizon is, the more time you have to grow your investments through compounding. It is recommended to stay invested for longer periods which will allow you time to ride out the short-term fluctuations in the market. A rule of thumb is to invest money which you can put aside for at least 5 years and more.

If you need your money in the short term, you should look for low-risk products that are easy to liquidate (e.g. fixed bonds).

- **How much money do you have to invest?**

It is always important to invest available disposable funds after accounting for your emergency fund, household expenses, insurance premiums, and short-term funds. Do not over-commit and invest funds which you may need in the short term.

- **How much risk can you take?**

Take note of your short-term and long-term needs – if you have more immediate needs, you should be taking on less risky investments. Also, if your investment suffers a loss, will it impact your other commitments, such as loan repayments? Do not take the risk if you do not have the time to recover from your losses. Be extra prudent when you are investing your retirement savings, especially since when you are already in your retirement years. On the flip side, if you are still young and have a longer time horizon, you can afford to take on more risk as an investor.

- **What are your investment goals?**

Work out how much money you need and when you need it for each of your financial goals. This will help you determine the returns you need to reach your goals. If you are just starting your career, your investment objective should be to grow your fund through capital appreciation, e.g. through stocks, etc.

If you have already reached your savings goal, your investment objective might then be to secure your capital through the fixed income. If you have retired and need to access your nest egg, you may also wish to earn a passive income from your investments such as receiving dividends.

A simple way of focusing your objectives is to decide which category you fall into – growth, income or capital preservation. Here's a sample of what it might look like:

	Growth Enhance your returns	Income Maximise your income	Security Preserve capital
Portfolio emphasis	Equity oriented	Fixed-income oriented	Fixed-income oriented
Return	High	Medium to high	Lower
Risk	High	Medium	Lower
Possible investments	Stocks, ETFs	Dividend-paying stocks, bonds	Bonds

For example, you might be in your twenties and are competent in investing, so you might want to go for index or value investing to grow your capital base more aggressively. As you approach your 40s and 50s, armed with a sizable investment fund, your focus might be more on capital preservation and generation of passive income. This might make dividend investing more suitable and appealing.

At the end of the day, you can choose to adopt whichever investment strategy you are comfortable with as long as it ultimately fulfills your goals and needs. And with that, let's go through the core investment strategies with deep fundamental analysis imparted by Buffett to begin your investment journey!

Chapter 11

Types Of Investing: Buffett Methodology

Finally, we can reveal the secret to achieving F.I.R.E!

Depending on whether you want to adopt an active or passive management of your investments, there are a few highly recommended strategies based on past proven and tested results which delivered sustainable and consistent returns (plus these are recommended by the Oracle of Omaha – Warren Buffett himself).

In Buffett's own words, he recommended investors to buy the index fund consistently at the lowest cost possible. It makes the most sense practically all the time – assuming you prefer the passive way of investing and do not wish to learn too much on stocks or how to do the fundamental analysis, etc.

The table on the next page shows that if you had invested US$100,000 in the S&P 500 index in 2008, it would have grown to US$207,608 by 2017. This makes it almost a total return of 107.6% or 11.9% annualized returns over the last 9 years.

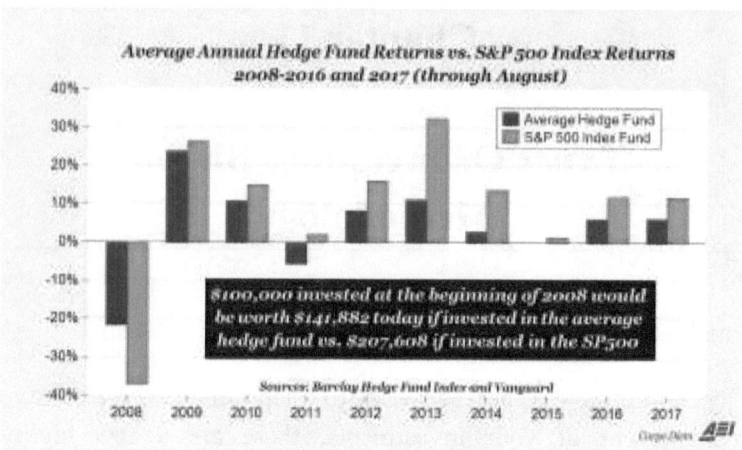

As one progresses along the investment journey, he/she might want to consider an active management of his/her investment which can potentially yield greater returns. Next, the other two investment strategies, which are closely tied to Buffett's investing approach, are dividends investing and value investing.

In 2019, Berkshire Hathaway will receive US$4,646,737,673 in dividend payments. This is one of Buffett's secrets.

Company Name	No. of Shares Owned	Annual Dividend Amount (US$)	Estimated Income (US$)
American Airlines Group	43,700,000	$0.40	$17,480,000

Company Name	No. of Shares Owned	Annual Dividend Amount (US$)	Estimated Income (US$)
Apple	252,478,779	$2.92	$737,238,035
American Express	151,610,700	$1.56	$236,512,692
Bank of America	877,248,600	$0.60	$526,349,160
Bank of NY Mellon	77,849,476	$1.12	$87,191,413
Costco Wholesale	4,333,363	$2.28	$9,880,068
Delta Air Lines	65,535,000	$1.40	$91,749,000
General Motors	52,461,411	$1.52	$79,741,345
Goldman Sachs	18,353,635	$3.20	$58,731,632

Company Name	No. of Shares Owned	Annual Dividend Amount (US$)	Estimated Income (US$)
JPMorgan Chase	35,664,767	$3.20	$114,127,254
Johnson & Johnson	327,100	$3.60	$1,177,560
Kraft Heinz (NASDAQ:KHC)	325,634,818	$2.50	$814,087,045
Coca-Cola	400,000,000	$1.56	$624,000,000
Southwest Airlines	56,047,339	$0.64	$35,870,297
Mastercard	4,934,756	$1.32	$6,513,878
Moody's Corp.	24,669,778	$1.76	$43,418,809
Mondelez International	578,000	$1.04	$601,120

Company Name	No. of Shares Owned	Annual Dividend Amount (US$)	Estimated Income (US$)
M&T Bank	5,382,040	$4.00	$21,528,160
Oracle	41,404,791	$0.76	$31,467,641
Procter & Gamble	315,400	$2.87	$905,198
PNC Financial Services	6,087,319	$3.80	$23,131,812
Phillips 66	15,433,024	$3.20	$49,385,677
Restaurant Brands Int'l	8,438,225	$1.80	$15,188,805
Sirius XM Holdings	137,915,729	$0.05	$6,895,786
Store Capital	18,621,674	$1.32	$24,580,610

Company Name	No. of Shares Owned	Annual Dividend Amount (US$)	Estimated Income (US$)
Synchrony Financial	20,803,000	$0.84	$17,474,520
Torchmark	6,353,727	$0.64	$4,066,385
Travelers Cos.	3,543,688	$3.08	$10,914,559
United Parcel Service	59,400	$3.64	$216,216
U.S. Bancorp	124,923,092	$1.48	$184,886,176
Visa	10,562,460	$1.00	$10,562,460
Verizon	928	$2.41	$2,236
Wells Fargo	442,361,700	$1.72	$760,862,124

DATA SOURCE: BERKSHIRE HATHAWAY 13-F, YAHOO! FINANCE.

In his latest annual letter to his shareholders, Buffett explained that his favorite dividend stocks do a lot more than just making regular dividend payout to the investors. They tend to add to stronger returns which had been enjoyed over a long time.

Why dividends matter for Berkshire Hathaway?

Buffett has explained why he likes stocks that pay dividends. As Buffett can deploy his investment to the best possible use, he use the dividends received and reinvest them. Similarly, you can either reinvest back into the stock that paid the dividends or you can also choose to reinvest them into other investment with better potential returns.

The other side of the coin

Though Buffett buys companies that give dividends, it is not the most important factor in his investing methodology. In his view, it is how those companies choose to use the bulk of money as retained earnings that is important.

In the latest shareholder letter, Buffett reveals the breakdown of Berkshire's five top holdings between what they pay in dividends and their retained earnings. His chart is reproduced here:

Stock	Berkshire's Stake	Berkshire Share of Dividends(US$)	Berkshire Share of Retained Earnings (US$)
American Express	17.9%	$237 million	$997 million
Apple	5.4%	$745 million	$2.50 billion
Bank of America	9.5%	$551 million	$2.10 billion
Coca-Cola	9.4%	$624 million	($21 million)
Wells Fargo	9.8%	$809 million	$1.26 billion

DATA SOURCE: BERKSHIRE HATHAWAY 2018 SHAREHOLDER LETTER.

All told, the amount Berkshire receives from these five holdings in dividends is US$2.97 billion per year. But retained earnings add up to more than twice as much - US$6.84 billion at last count.

Why are retained earnings more valuable than dividends?

First, over time, the retained earnings produced a large contribution to Berkshire's overall returns on investment – all of his companies have generated capital gains that exceeded the value of their reinvested funds.

Even better, Buffett likes companies that take a portion of their retained earnings to buy back its shares. When a company buys back its shares, the investor's stake in that company goes up without it having to buy a single share.

For an investor who prefers owning big chunks of great companies rather than small positions, repurchases help Buffett achieve his goals. And where there are dividends, there are often buybacks, especially in the current investing environment.

Value investing

And of course, let's not forget the hallmark strategy for the Berkshire Hathaway Chairman and CEO Warren Buffett, which is the classic value investing style. In fact, Buffett invests using a more qualitative and concentrated approach which is to focus on quality businesses that have reasonable valuations and potential for large growth.

Essentially, it is to assess the intrinsic value which is the underlying fair value of a stock based on its future earnings.

Fundamental analysis of investing

The ring to rule them all! Yes, the shining light, which guides you through all the Buffett's investing strategies, requires fundamental analysis. The use of fundamental analysis is a very grounded and traditional approach to investing. The main rule of fundamental analysis is to first understand how a company or business operates and creates value at a fundamental level.

This involves studying the company's historical financial statements, as well as the competitive landscape and regulatory influences, amongst other things. What will happen to this company's revenue and profit for the next few years? What happens if a competitor tries to take its market share with an aggressive pricing strategy?

By attempting these kinds of questions, an investor seeks to assess the true 'fair intrinsic value' of a company by evaluating and investing in a company whose stock price deviates the most from its fair value. Acquiring this fundamental analysis approach will serve you well as a strong investing foundation to bring along in your investment journey to build wealth!

Chapter 12

Index Investing

In Warren Buffett's 2016 letter to Berkshire Hathaway shareholders, he mentioned, "if a statue is ever erected to honor the person who has done the most for American investors, the hands-down choice should be Jack Bogle."

Jack Bogle, the founder of the Vanguard Company, created the first index fund in 1976. He wanted to create a way to invest passively instead of using the mutual fund managers who were trying to outperform the market – his research found there's no way for a mutual fund to consistently outperform the market long term but they can consistently underperform the market due to excessive costs, e.g. management fees, etc.

The beauty of the index fund is that it allows an average investor to invest very inexpensively while achieving market results.

What is an index?

An index is a list of stocks or bonds traded, e.g. the Standard & Poor's 500 (S&P 500) is a list of the top 500 stocks traded on the New York Stock Exchange by market capitalization which is based on the total dollar market value of a company's outstanding share. S&P 500 has also been recommended by Buffett himself for passive investors to acquire in their portfolio.

In general, there are also other indexes that track just about everything. There are those that can mirror the equities based on market capitalization (large, mid-cap, or small), sector (e.g. biotech, technology), regions (e.g. Europe, emerging markets), stock exchange (e.g. Nasdaq, Nikkei, STI), and even indexes that attempt to track the entire global stock market.

Generally, the financial news will almost always focus on the performance of the S&P 500 index, the Dow Jones Industrial Average, and the Nasdaq 100 index.

Why do index investing?

Investing in index funds or exchange-traded funds (ETFs) may sound more boring than investing in carefully chosen individual stocks, but these funds have a solid track record. Over the last 15 years ending in June 2018, about 92% of U.S. large-cap stock mutual funds lagged the returns of the S&P 500.

One of the reasons why a passive investor can generate strong returns is the low fees generally. A typical mutual fund might carry an annual fee (expense ratio) of 1 to 3% or more, while many broad market index funds have an expense ratio of 0.25% and lower. It's important to note how much of a difference a single percentage point of expense fees can affect the outcome of the overall returns over a long-term period.

Supposed we have two identical mutual funds, one with an annual fee of 1.1% and the other charging 0.1%. The table shows the comparison in the rate of return if we have allowed the annual investment of US$10,000 to grow with an average return of 10% annually, and with those two fees subtracted:

No. of years	Rate of return at 8.9%	Rate of return at 9.9%
10 years	$164,663	$174,315
20 years	$550,920	$622,348
30 years	$1.5 million	$1.8 million

Even for the 1% difference in the annual fees, it shows that this adds up quickly in a large portfolio and can significantly eat into your returns; in this case, it was close to US$300,000 over a 30-year period. This large difference can be especially important when you are considering getting a fund manager who might put your money into a bunch of actively managed mutual funds. Not only will you have to pay the higher expense ratio for actively managed funds, plus not forgetting the additional asset management fees, even when the market or fund is not doing well. If you don't want to pay those fees, then investing in the index funds can provide a simple way just as fine.

For passive investors, index investing aims to generate the same returns as the market index through investing in low-cost ETFs that mirror the index. So if the market index (e.g. S&P 500) goes up by 10% in a year, you can expect to make similar returns. Over the time of inception of the market indexes like the S&P 500, the stock market has always risen over the long term period.

The advantage of this strategy is that if you want to be a passive investor who doesn't have the time and effort to stock pick, you can simply buy the whole market index instead. Investing in the index funds or ETFs is one of the simplest ways to grow your wealth over time. For someone who's not interested in researching individual companies to put together a balanced and diversified portfolio themselves, index funds are the best investment tool available.

In fact, you may think to yourself that even Buffett himself will recommend investing in index funds, but has he actually put his own money where his mouth is? Well yes he has, through a famous 10-year US$1million bet that recently concluded (he won it, by the way, having bet that index funds would outperform hedge funds over a decade).

What's the difference between index funds and ETFs?

As we were sharing earlier, when you want to buy an index fund, you will come across exchange-traded fund (ETFs) which is merely a subset of index funds that trade more like equities. An ETF is traded on an exchange with a constant fluctuating price. Investors can buy shares just like a stock, which means no fractional shares, but they can buy as few as one share.

Often, ETFs tends to have lower expense ratios than similar index mutual funds. For example, the Vanguard Total Stock Market ETF has an expense ratio of just 0.04%. On the other hand, the Vanguard Total Stock Market Index Fund Investor Shares mutual fund has an expense ratio of 0.14% which is 10 percentage points higher.

Given that ETFs are traded like stocks, it is easy to sell an ETF which means there is high liquidity, similar to other stocks.

How to invest in the index funds or index ETFs?

Many index funds also appear in the ETF format, where they trade like stocks, but are essentially index funds.

Here are some index funds ETFs to consider:

Code	Name	What it tracks	Country listed	Inception	Expense Ratio	5-year Return
ES3	SPDR Straits Times Index ETF (ES3.SI)	STI	SG	2002	0.30%	3.73%
EEM	iShares MSCI Emerging Markets ETF (EEM	Emerging Markets	U.S.	2003	0.69%	4.31%
IWDA	iShares Core MSCI World ETF USD Acc	World	Ireland	2009	0.20%	7.97%
VT	Vanguard Total World Stock ETF (VT)	World	U.S.	2008	0.10%	10.44%
URTH	iShares MSCI World ETF (URTH)	World	U.S.	2012	0.24%	10.60%
SWDA	iShares Core MSCI World UCITS ETF USD (Acc)	World	Ireland	2010	0.20%	12.20%
SWPPX	Schwab S&P 500 Index (SWPPX)	S&P 500	U.S.	1997	0.05%	12.40%

Code	Name	What it tracks	Country listed	Inception	Expense Ratio	5-year Return
VOO	Vanguard S&P 500 ETF (VOO)	S&P 500	U.S.	2010	0.04%	12.42%
IVV	iShares Core S&P 500 ETF (IVV)	S&P 500	U.S.	2000	0.05%	12.42%
DIA	SPDR® Dow Jones Industrial Average ETF	Dow Jones 30	U.S.	1998	0.17%	13.24%
CSPX	iShares Core S&P 500 UCITS ETF USD (Acc)	S&P 500	Ireland	2011	0.07%	16.54%
QQQ	Invesco QQQ Trust (QQQ)	Nasdaq 100	U.S.	1999	0.20%	18.36%

From the table above, here are some quick tips:

- Don't invest in the STI index ETF

- S&P 500 index ETF has outperformed the World index ETF

- Nasdaq 100 index ETF has outperformed the S&P500 index ETF

How to select an index ETF:

You can start by considering some of the index ETFs in the table above. The returns of the S&P 500 index ETF can be used as a benchmark recommended by Buffett. If you want to gain higher returns than the S&P 500 index ETF, you may consider the Nasdaq 100 index ETF which can generate over 18% annualized returns.

One consideration will be the year of the inception. You may want to look at an index ETF which has been in the market over 8 to 10 years. You will be able to view the 10 years or 15 years annualized returns of the index ETF using Morningstar.com website.

Of course, most of the index ETFs are below 1% which are already very good.

Under 'country listed', you will see U.S. and Ireland. This refers to the country stock exchange the index ETF is listed on. For those listed on the U.S. stock exchange, there is a 30% withholding tax on dividends, while those listed on the London Stock Exchange or are Ireland domiciled, are given a lower 15% withholding tax on dividends.

You can buy most of these index ETFs using your local brokerages but do check out the fees for holding a foreign counter. For U.S. index ETFs, you may want to buy it from a U.S. brokerage. For those who may want to invest in the SG market (including buying some U.S. index ETF listed on LSE), you may buy them from a local brokerage.

Again, if you are someone who enjoys researching individual stocks and wants to have higher returns, then you may want to look at other investing strategies shared in the later chapters. You don't need to own 500 stocks to have a diversified portfolio!

But for someone who is not interested and just wants to grow their money at the average annualized returns based on the market index, you can go with index or ETFs investing.

Chapter 13

Income / Dividend Investing

What is dividend investing?

For people who love to see money flowing into their bank account every year or quarter, dividend investing can be an excellent way to generate income and grow their investment portfolio over a long period of time. By focusing on fundamentally strong companies that pay out dividends regularly, the reinvestment can be turned into a large investment chest with compounded gains.

Why invest in dividend stocks?

Dividend-paying companies tend to be more mature and stable than their non-dividends counterparts and this allows a solid portfolio of dividend stocks to create massive amounts of wealth over a long period of time. As such, these stocks or REITs (Real Estate Investment Trust) are worth buying and holding on to over an extended time period for investors of all ages.

Many people actually invest in dividend stocks to reinvest the dividend payment by purchasing additional shares of company stock. Since these companies tend to be financially stable, the stock price tends to increase steadily over time while increasing dividend payments are still distributed – a win-win for investors. E.g. Coca-Cola paid US$1.40 dividend in 2016 and

US$1.48 in 2017. There may be no guarantees. A company that has earned a reputation for delivering reliable dividends over time is going to work doubly hard to keep its strong track record.

Adding to the point of being fundamentally stable, those dividend stocks tend to be less volatile than the market in general. As such, they may be of lower risk than companies that don't pay dividends. Stocks which pay dividends tend to be of lower risk. They can appeal to younger people who are looking for ways to grow their wealth over the long period of time, as well as older people who may want passive income flow in their retirement years.

How to do dividend investing?

For the dividend investing, the goal is to be able to invest enough into a dividend portfolio so that the dividends you receive each year can cover your yearly expenses.

To start building the dividend portfolio, you will need to identify solid companies or REITs with a strong track record of paying stable dividends increasingly each year. When you decide to invest into dividend stocks, you should monitor your investment closely. This is because dividend stocks may carry a risk that is unique to itself, such as its management team doing a bad job, or losing to its competitors, etc. We will look into how to select your dividend stocks later.

For the Singapore market, you can invest in blue-chip companies. They are often large and stable companies with a strong track record of positive business earnings and dividend payout. These are strong indicators of their business performance. You will also need to review their cash flow and payout ratio to see if the company's earnings and cash flow can support the dividend payout in a sustainable manner.

In recent times, REITs have been very popular as they are required by regulations to pay over 90% of their profits back to the shareholders. This provides a strong visibility into the timing and amount of future dividends being paid.

The table below shows the investment portfolio size you need to have based on the percentage of dividend yield, in order to achieve a specific dividend amount each year to sustain your expenses.

Total dividend amount required each year	Investment Portfolio size with X% dividend yield				
	3%	5%	6%	7%	8%
$6,000	$200,000	$120,000	$100,000	$85,714.29	$75,000
$12,000	$400,000	$240,000	$200,000	$171,428.57	$150,000
$14,400	$480,000	$288,000	$240,000	$205,714.29	$180,000
$24,000	$800,000	$480,000	$400,000	$342,857.14	$300,000
$37,068	$1,235,600	$741,360	$617,800	$529,542.86	$463,350
$56,388	$1,879,600	$1,127,760	$939,800	$805,542.86	$704,850
$120,000	$4,000,000	$2,400,000	$2,000,000	$1,714,285.71	$1,500,000

Why is the Singapore market good for dividend investing?

- One of the key factors is that there isn't any tax on capital gains and dividends. In the U.S. market, if you are a non-U.S. investor, you will be taxed 30% on withholding tax (related to dividends), and estate tax, etc.

- Another reason is that the Singapore market provides the best environment to build a dividend portfolio which includes dividend stocks and Real Estate Investment Trust (REITs) and can generate returns in times of rising or declining interest rates, etc.

How to select dividend stocks?

When it comes to selecting dividend stocks, one of the key factors will be to assess the fundamental strength of the company and its ability to pay consistent dividends. This is an indicator on the financial standing of the stock and how it can perform in future.

For example, a company which aims to increase its dividends at an increasing rate may be in a relatively strong financial position. The management team could be anticipating a rise in its profitability over a period of time which can justify a high dividends growth. As investors, we may prefer to see both the stock price appreciating and receive passive dividend income from the investment each year.

If you are more of an income investor and prefer to invest for dividends, your stock portfolio will be different from someone investing for high growth and capital gains. Do note that the stocks which provide you consistent dividends may not necessarily be the type that will grow by 20 to 40% a year. Now, the question is: how can you select the best stocks that will pay passive dividends?

Here are some factors to consider when picking out dividend stocks:

   a.   Search for mid to large-cap stocks

The best dividend stocks tend to be large and mature companies with stable revenue, profits, and cash flow. These companies may not grow as much and are not expanding aggressively. Hence, the majority of the earnings are returned back to the shareholders as dividends.

   b.   The dividend payout ratio is 50% or more

Aim to look for a company with a dividend payout ratio of at least 50% or more. If the company has a low payout ratio, we will need to ask ourselves why the company is holding onto the cash. Unless the company has a good reason to hold or reinvest the cash, the majority of the profits should be paid out.

   c.   Good past performance record of consistent dividends

The company should have a long and stable performance record of paying dividends to shareholders consistently. One way is to look the dividend payout over the last 5 to 10 years. There should be a steady increase pattern in the payout rate. This shows that as the company grows more profitable, the management is also willing to give back more to the shareholders.

d. Ensure that the company's fundamentals are solid and sustainable

We will need to evaluate the company using the fundamental analysis. Many dividend investors tend to ignore the overall aspect of the company's fundamentals and focus on the dividend yield, which may be insufficient. While it is good to evaluate the dividend yield, it is also important to consider the overall health of the company. A company with deteriorating fundamentals (e.g. declining revenue, profits, cash flow, etc.) cannot sustain its dividend payout in the long term. The less revenue and profits the company makes, the less dividend it can pay out eventually. Over time, should you buy into a company with a dividend payout but has declining fundamentals, you will encounter the falling of its stock price. This fall in value will eat into any dividend gains which you have accumulated at the start, leaving you back to square one or even worse off.

So always make sure the dividend company you want to invest in will remain fundamentally strong and robust for many years to come.

e. The company should have low CAPEX

As a dividend investor, you may prefer companies with low capital expenditure (CAPEX). A company with high CAPEX means it has to continually reinvest its profits to maintain its business operations, leaving less funds for dividend payout. So do look for a company that is able to maintain or grow its business with minimal CAPEX.

f. Company has a stable growing cash flow

The company must have real cash to pay the dividends to its shareholders. Do check if the earnings or free cash flow per share is more than the dividends per share. If the company is profitable but has negative or inconsistent free cash flow, it will have trouble paying stable dividends. A smaller company that is seeking to grow might have negative free cash flow as it expands its business. But a large and stable company should be producing high amounts of free cash flow year on year. If not, you will need to further understand why.

g. Dividend yield should be higher than the risk free rate

The dividend yield you receive should ideally beat the risk-free rate in the country you're living in. In the U.S., the risk-free rate is usually based on the 10-year U.S. Treasury note which is around 2.5%. In Singapore, the risk-free rate is usually based on the interest of the Central Provident Fund (CPF) Special Account which can give you about 4%. If the dividend stock that you have chosen cannot even beat the risk-free rate, then you might as well put the money into the your CPF or the U.S. treasury notes to grow the funds.

Here are the selection criteria riding on the fundamental analysis:

	Selection Criteria
1	Market Capitalization: more than $10 billion
2	Debt to Equity Ratio: less than 1 or below 0.5
3	Return on Equity (ROE): more than 10%
4	Earnings per share (EPS) growth last 5 years: positive trend
5	Profit margins %: more than 10%
6	Revenue growth % last 10 years: positive trend
7	Net income growth % last 10 years: positive trend
8	Profit growth % last 10 years: positive trend
9	Dividend yield: more than 4% and the dividend payout trend should be positive or growing steadily
10	Payout ratio: more than 50% but less than 100%. Is the earnings per share or free cash flow per share greater than the dividends per share?
11	The ROE trend in the past 5 to 10 years should be positive
12	The Operating Cash Flow trend in the past 5 to 10 years should be positive
13	The Net Income trend in the past 5 to 10 years should be positive

You can extract these data and populate the key financial figures and numbers onto into a spreadsheet and then filter the stocks.

What are REITs?

If you are looking for some stable, passive income, REITs will be a great addition to enhance your investment portfolio.

REITs are listed companies that pool investors' capital to invest, own and operate real estate properties. The properties are leased to tenants for rent. Investors who invest in REITs are similar to being co-owners of the REITs.

REITs can be traded in the stock market. Due to the unique structure, REITs allow investors to gain exposure to the property market with little funds. REITs will generate income from renting and selling of assets, so the money earned is paid out to the shareholders through distribution, e.g. dividends.

REITs enjoy a unique tax transparency structure treatment, unlike common stocks, whereby REITs are required to pay at least 90% of their taxable income (in the case of Singapore). These high dividend payouts make Singapore REITs very attractive and are seen as a viable option and strong dividend player for investors who love passive income. As the property market appreciates, the prices of the REITs will go up and allow additional capital gains on top of the dividend payout.

To show what the average REIT returns is like, we take the widely used Singapore REIT index, which consists of 20 largest and most traded REITs in Singapore, that delivers on average 11% annualized total return over the past 5 years. Based on the REITs listed in Singapore, you can enjoy an average dividend yield of 5% to 8% a year, which is paid quarterly or every 6 months.

Types of REITs

In general, there are a few key types of REITs in Singapore which are Healthcare, Commercial, Industrial, Hospitality, and Retail.

- Healthcare

Healthcare REITs make investments in healthcare facilities which include hospitals, nursing homes and assisted living properties. With Singapore facing an aging but more affluent population, the healthcare sector will become more important in servicing the needs of the elderly. As the demand for healthcare rises, infrastructure to support the healthcare facilities will be key.

Examples: Parkway Life REIT, First REIT

- Commercial

Commercial REITs make investment in office REITs, and these REITs have many office buildings under their company, e.g. Capital Tower, HSBC building, Twenty Anson, etc. Currently, the supply of office spaces outstrips the demand, so commercial REITs might not attract the interest of some retail investors. However, do note that co-working spaces are becoming increasingly popular, especially for smaller companies. This is to maximize the utilization of the office space. Given more businesses are moving out to business parks and areas outside of the city center, investors might want to look at REITs in those areas.

Examples: Capitaland Commercial Trust, Frasers Commercial Trust

- Industrial

Industrial REITs own facilities that are used for industrial purposes such as factories, warehouses, manufacturing sites, and business parks. Industrial REITs are influenced by the manufacturing sector, and the spaces can be converted for various needs. These areas tend to be outside of the CBD centers.

Examples: Ascendas REIT, Mapletree Industrial Trust, Viva Industrial Trust

- Hospitality

Hospitality REITs invest in properties such as hotels and serviced residences. Hotels in the hospitality sector are also dependent on tourist arrivals. With the constant stream of tourists into the country, the hospitality industry seems to be attracting investors. However, do note that tourism is greatly affected by general news and economic downturn.

Examples: Ascendas Hospitality Trust, Ascott Residence Trust, CDL Hospitality Trust

- Retail

Retail REITs invest in shopping malls such as Raffles City, Bugis Junction, ION Orchard, etc. Retail REITs tend to be popular among retail investors as it is relatively easier to understand how they work. Retail investors can also do their site inspection by going to the respective malls to observe the foot traffic. In recent years, with the growth of e-commerce, the physical retail space in Singapore has been declining.

However, shopping malls, especially heartland malls, will not go obsolete as Singaporeans will still need to get some necessities or food at the mall.

Examples: Capitaland Mall Trust, Frasers Centrepoint Trust

How to select REITs?

We have established that REITs can also offer a form of passive income and covered the various types of REITs. We will touch on some of the key areas to look out for when selecting the REITs.

a.   REITs should not be overvalued

While REITs have a different structure to the traditional real estate investment structure, REITs are an investment which will depend on the ability of the underlying real estate to generate income. Hence, the valuation of the REIT is crucial.

b.   REITs need to have a good general outlook

Before we invest in the REITs, we will also need to see which of the sub-sector has a good investment outlook. The outlook can be referred to any macro trends from interest rate, regulatory trends to industry and economic trends. For example, if we know that the global economy is slowing down, this may indirectly impact the rental market in the office REIT industry, leading to negative rental reversion.

c.   REITs need to show growth factor

REITs are also similar to the nature of stocks. The REIT owns a portfolio of properties and receives income from these properties, which are then distributed as dividends to shareholders, just like dividend stocks. Also, the REITs price can appreciate, similar to stocks, where the growth outlooks can push the share price higher. Good REITs tend to grow the net income year-on-year.

The growth can be in terms of organic growth through Asset Enhancement Initiatives (AEIs), positive rental reversion and growing occupancy or through inorganic growth through the acquisition of new properties.

d.   REITs need to have a good capitalization rate and not just good dividend yield

For REITs, we will look at the Capitalization rate or Cap Rate, which is the rate of return on a real estate investment property based on the income that the property is expected to generate. Do note that this Cap Rate is not the same as distribution yield – the Cap Rate measures the REIT's income yielding ability against the underlying asset value while the distribution yield measures a REIT's income against the market capitalization.

A high Cap Rate can signal that the management or property can command a higher rental income. This gives you an indication on whether the REITs can generate a good rental income.

Here are the selection criteria when choosing fundamentally strong REITs:

	Selection Criteria
1	Market Capitalization
2	Price/Net Asset Value (NAV): close to 1 or below
3	Occupancy Rate above 95%: shows how well the REITs manage the tenants
4	Weighted Average Lease Expiry (WALE) above 2 years: the longer the WALE, the longer the secured rental income
5	Net Operating Income: should have a positive trend over 3 to 5 years
6	Capitalization Rate/Cap Rate %: should be above 7%
7	Dividend Yield %: should be above 5%
8	Return on Equity (ROE): should be above 10%
9	Gearing Ratio (similar to debt ratio): should be lower than 35%
10	Annualized Return %: should be above 10%
11	Distribution Per Unit (DPU): should see a positive growing trend over 3 to 5 years
12	Profit Margin % or Profit: should see a positive growing trend over 3 to 5 years

Once you have selected the list of REITs, you will need to look at the Price/NAV to decide the entry point. If the Price/NAV is above 1, it is considered overvalued. When the Price/NAV is close to 1 or below, it is considered undervalued.

For REITs, do you know that we can generate double-digit yield?

One example is Mapletree Commercial Trust (MCT), which holds a portfolio of retail and office properties.

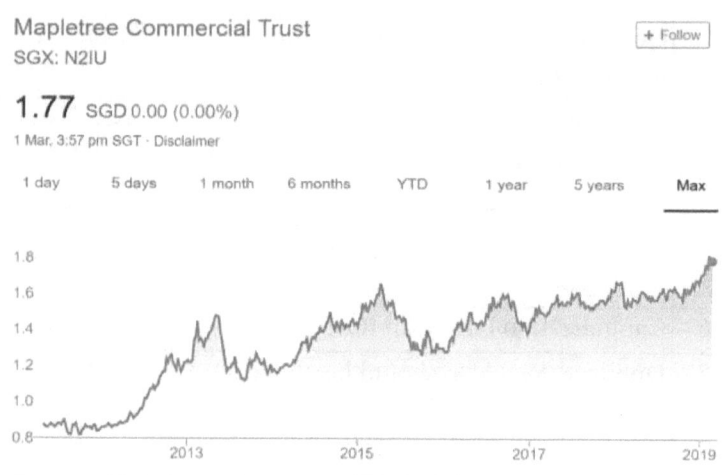

Chart: Google Finance

From the charts, it also shows the capital appreciation for the REIT itself which adds to the overall returns.

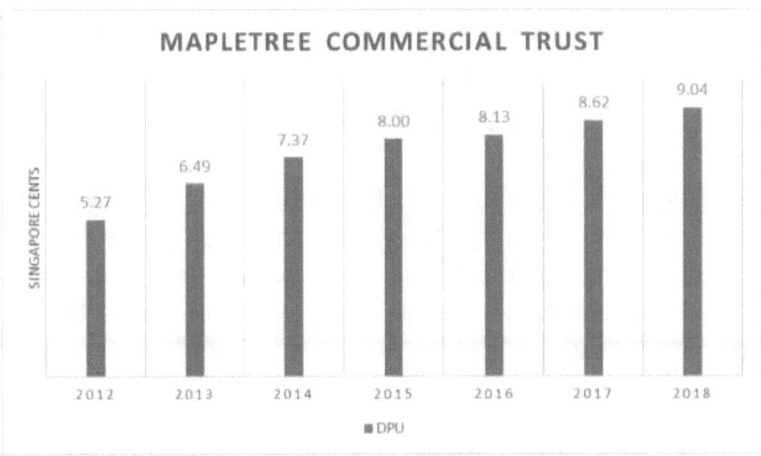

Source: Mapletree Commercial Trust

The above is a chart of MCT's distribution per unit (DPU) over the last seven years. As you can see, MCT has grown its DPU by 71.5% since its listing from 5.27 cents in 2012 to 9.04 cents in 2018.

It also shows how a successful company or REIT can continue to grow its dividend payout over the years. Overall, we can gain not only the dividends payout but also in capital gains from a fundamentally strong REIT like MCT.

Why invest in REITs in Singapore?

a.   Safe and stable environment

Singapore is a safe and stable place to live in and investors dare to invest in the country to drive economic growth. This can also, in return, help to increase the value of the properties in Singapore given the demand. Also, land space is limited in

Singapore so property prices will continue to rise in future. Investing in REITs is a great way to invest in properties.

b. Tax-free environment

In Singapore, investing in REITs can give high yields due to the incentive given by the government, e.g. REITs are not required to pay the usual 17% corporate tax rate if it pays 90% of its distributable income to investors as dividends. Due to this, REITs can earn a higher income and can afford to provide higher dividend payout.

c. Well-diversification

Assuming you own a physical property on your own, this means the risk is concentrated in one property or area. On the other hand, a REIT owns a range of real estate ranging from malls, offices, industrial, etc. Hence, your risk is more diversified.

For example, Frasers Centrepoint Trust (FCT) owns malls like Centrepoint, Causeway Point, Changi City Point which are diversified island-wide. Since its listing in 2007, FCT has netted cumulative dividends of around 68%, including capital gains. If you invested S$10,000, you would have netted S$6,800 in dividends alone.

d. Tight regulation

In Singapore, the Monetary Authority of Singapore (MAS) under the Collective Investment Scheme (CIS) of Securities and Future (SFA) Act governs Singapore REITs. MAS regulations state that a REIT's total borrowings cannot exceed 35% of its total assets. In addition, REITs are not allowed to spend more than 25% of its total asset value on new developments so the risk of REITs defaulting on its debt is low and managed at a regulatory level. Despite being well-regulated, there are some cases whereby a REIT manager can also mismanage a REIT and lead it to financial trouble.

e. High Yield

As shared earlier, some REITs can achieve an average 11% annualized total return and produce dividend yield of 6% to 8%. However, we will need a proper investment methodology to select the fundamentally strong REITs in Singapore. REITs pay dividends up to 4 times a year. The yields from REITs are higher as compared to bonds and fixed deposit and they also have the potential for capital growth, hence increasing the overall gains.

Red flags for REITs?

- REITs are highly leveraged

The Monetary Authority of Singapore has mandated REITs to have a gearing ratio of 45%. This gearing ratio is calculated by taking the REIT's total borrowings and dividing it by its total assets. Generally, it will be good for REITs to have the ratio below 35% to have some buffer. If the REITs' gearing ratio is 35% and above, there might not be any safety margin when there is a sudden economic downturn. If that happens, the REITs will have to raise funds through ways such as a rights issue or private placement to bring down the gearing ratio.

- REITs having excessive private placements

When the REIT sells its units to a specific group of investors, this is called private placements. Unlike a rights issue where the retail investors can participate in, private placements are reserved for a select group of investors such as institutional investors.

For example, CapitaLand Commercial trust conducted a private placement exercise and raised proceeds of S$217 million to fund a new acquisition in Germany. The issue price was at a discount of around 3% to the volume weighted average price for the REIT and this can be seen as diluting the existing unit-holders' share in the REIT. The more private placements are conducted, the more unit-holders' stakes are diluted.

- REITs have declining distribution per unit (DPU)

I shared earlier that you should be looking at growing DPU trend, and if the REIT's DPU is declining, it shows that the REIT may be having difficulties in increasing its rents and its prospects are likely not that great. One example is AIMS AMP Capital Industrial REIT, whose DPU has been declining due to headwinds and its dividend yield is at 7.3% shows that the dividend payout is not sustainable. When investing in REITs, you have to see the DPU trend and not just based on dividend yield alone.

- REITs have a high valuation

There are a few ways to see the valuation of the REITs. Generally, you should avoid Price to NAV being above 1. This means the REIT is trading at a premium to its net asset value. You will always want to buy the REIT when it is near to the fair or undervalued price range. It will be good to get REITs with dividend yield of 6% to commensurate with the risk taken to hold them. REITs are riskier instrument in general due to the high borrowing costs and if the credit freezes during a downturn, it can be tough.

Some of Warren Buffett's dividend stocks:

Wells Fargo (WFC)

Percent of Warren Buffett's Portfolio: 10.7%
Dividend Yield: 3.7%   **Forward P/E Ratio:** 9.9x   (as of 2/18/19)
Sector: Financials   **Industry:** Major Regional Banks
Dividend Growth Streak: 8 years

Coca-Cola (KO)

Percent of Warren Buffett's Portfolio: 10.4%
Dividend Yield: 3.5%   **Forward P/E Ratio:** 21.6x   (as of 2/18/19)
Sector: Consumer Staples   **Industry:** Soft Drinks
Dividend Growth Streak: 56 years

Does Warren Buffet invest for dividends?

One of the longtime misunderstandings is that though Buffett often invests in stocks that pay dividends to their shareholders, Buffett has never opted for Berkshire to pay a dividend. In the 2018 annual letter to shareholders, Buffett explained that the dividend stocks do more than just dividends payout to investors and they make very smart investment to add to the strong returns for Berkshire to enjoy over time.

In 2018, the company received US$3.8 billion in dividends, and Buffett said the amount of dividends Berkshire gets in 2019 should be higher than that.

Wow! With that amount of dividends, Buffett still holds the view that it is far more important to note how his investments (the companies' stocks that he owns) use the bulk of their retained earnings for efficient returns. In the latest shareholder letter, Buffett spoke of Berkshire's five top holdings and gave a breakdown of the dividends they pay and their retained earnings.

His chart is reproduced as follows:

Company Name	Berkshire Hathaway's Stake	Berkshire Hathaway's Share of Dividends (US$)	Berkshire Hathaway's Share of Retained Earnings (US$)
American Express	17.9%	$237 million	$997 million
Apple	5.4%	$745 million	$2.50 billion
Bank of America	9.5%	$551 million	$2.10 billion
Coca-Cola	9.4%	$624 million	($21 million)

Company Name	Berkshire Hathaway's Stake	Berkshire Hathaway's Share of Dividends (US$)	Berkshire Hathaway's Share of Retained Earnings (US$)
Wells Fargo	9.8%	$809 million	$1.26 billion

DATA SOURCE: BERKSHIRE HATHAWAY 2018 SHAREHOLDER LETTER.

Even though Berkshire received about US$2.97 billion per year from these 5 holdings, the retained earnings are almost twice as much as US$6.84 billion.

What Buffett thinks about retained earnings being more valuable than dividends?

Buffett explains the two reasons why he prefers the value of retained earnings as his top investment. First, the retained earnings have contributed significantly to Berkshire's overall returns on investment. All of his companies have generated capital gains that exceeded the value of their reinvested capital.

Buffett also likes it when companies use their retained earnings to buy back shares. This allows Berkshire's stake in the underlying company to go up without having to buy a single share. For an investor who prefers owning a large portion of great companies than small positions, repurchases can help Buffett achieve that. When there is a dividend payout, there will also be buybacks.

Chapter 14

Value Investing

What is value investing?

Finally, we are at the most important cornerstone of the whole Buffett investing strategy which is value investing.

Buffett invests by looking for fundamentally strong stocks which are undervalued by the market or stocks which are valuable but not recognized by the market. He is also not concerned with the supply and demand of the stock market. In fact, there is a famous quote by him, "In the short term, the market is a popularity contest; in the long term it is a weighing machine."

Buffett chooses stocks based on their overall potential as a company and he plans to hold them as a long-term strategy. He is only concerned about owning good quality companies which are extremely capable of generating consistently strong earnings.

For value investing, you are not required to have an extensive background in Finance although understanding the basics will definitely help. If you have common sense, patience, money to invest and the willingness to do some reading and effort to execute the buy, you can become a value investor. Here are 5 fundamental concepts you will need to understand before getting started:

Value Investing Fundamental Number 1: All companies have intrinsic value

The basic concept behind value investing is a simple idea that if we can assess the true value of something, we can save a lot of money when we buy that item on sales or on discounts. The stock price of the company may change according to the demand even when the company's intrinsic value still remains the same. The fluctuations change the prices but they don't really change what you're getting in terms of the value, unless the company innovates or radically changes its business fundamentals which may then change the intrinsic value. If you are willing to do the detective work to uncover some of these secret sales or companies priced under the value, you can get stocks at bargain prices that other investors will be oblivious to.

Value Investing Fundamental Number 2: Always have a margin of safety

One thing about buying stocks at bargain prices is that it gives you a higher chance of earning a profit when you sell and there is a higher runway for capital appreciation. The principle of the margin of safety is one of the key factors to successful value investing. For speculative or penny stocks whose prices may drop, it is less likely for value stocks to experience continuous decline provided there are strong track records.

If a stock is worth US$100 and you buy it for US$60, you will make a profit of US$40 simply by waiting for the stock's price to rise to the US$100 it's really worth. In addition to that, the company might grow, becoming more valuable and giving you a chance to make even more money. If the stock's price rises to US$110, you will make US$50 since you bought the stock on a sale. If you had purchased it at its full price of US$100, you would only make a US$10 profit. One way is to buy the stock when they are priced at two-thirds or less of their intrinsic value. This creates a margin of safety which allows a value investor to earn the best possible returns while reducing the potential downside.

Value Investing Fundamental Number 3: The efficient market hypothesis is wrong

Value investors don't believe in the efficient market theory which refers to the stock prices factoring in all information about the company and showing the right value technically. In reality, value investors tend to believe that the stocks are underpriced or overpriced in relation to their intrinsic value due to market irrationality. For instance, a stock might be underpriced because the economy is crashing or there is bad news about the company. Investors can go on a panic mode and start to sell the stocks, causing the price to decline. Or it might be overpriced because many investors or the market are overly confident about the future growth of a company that hasn't proven itself yet.

Value Investing Fundamental Number 4: Successful Investors don't follow the herd

One of the hallmark characteristics of a value investor is that they tend to be like contrarians – they don't like to follow the herd (we will discuss later that we also shouldn't follow Buffett's portfolio blindly). When everyone else is selling, they are buying or holding. Value investors don't tend to buy the most popular stocks in the current market because they're typically overpriced, but they are willing to invest in fundamentally strong companies if the financials show. Of course when the stock market crashes and while people are selling, value investors will go in to look and acquire those stocks with household names when the prices have declined. This is because value investors believe the fundamentally strong stocks can recover from the setbacks or after the crash.

Value investors will also focus on the stock's intrinsic value. This allows them to assess when to acquire and own a company that they know has sound principles and financials, regardless of what the rest of people / market / analysts say or do.

Value Investing Fundamental Number 5: Investing requires diligence and patience

These are fundamentally key concepts and attributes every value investor must have: due diligence and patience. Value investing is a long-term strategy and it doesn't give fast money (although I will touch on one of the investment techniques practiced by Warren Buffett to generate cash flow). E.g. for most of the valued stocks, it will be hard for the investor to buy it at US$60 on Monday and expect it to rise to US$100 by Friday (this is not like Cryptocurrency).

The thing about value investing is that it can be a bit of an art. Sometimes when you assess a stock to be fundamentally strong, you have to wait because it may be overpriced. The key is to buy the stock when the price is relatively attractive to its intrinsic value. Sometimes when none of the selected stocks are priced fairly or are undervalued, the value investor will then choose not to buy anything; he / she basically does nothing. Sometimes doing nothing can reap huge potential benefits.

How do we do value investing?

The key approach to value investing is to thoroughly research the company (which will be shown to you in a bit on how to fast track the research) and not just because the stock looks cheap. We will have to think about the company's prospects: Can the company increase its revenue by raising prices? Increasing sales? Lowering expenses or debt? Selling more profitably? Is the company growing? What is the economic moat of the company? Is there any brand equity?

To increase the odds of winning, it is wise to buy companies that you understand and that is to invest within your circle of competence. It could be companies that you are interested in, have worked for or that sell consumer goods or services which you are familiar with. Another strategy that value investor can use is to buy companies whose products or services have been in demand for a long time and should likely continue to be in demand. It may also be worthwhile to analyze the company's management and how they react to the changing business environments. A firm with a track record of evolving with the times may be a good bet.

Where can we then find all these information as a value investor?

A wealth of information can be found in the financial reports which present the company's annual and quarterly performance results. Companies are required to file these reports with the Securities and Exchange Commission (SEC). You can find out lots of information from the company's annual report, which explains the products and/or services the company sells and gives you a good idea of how the company operates and sees itself.

The company's financial report will provide the data that you as an investor will want to analyze such as revenue, operating expenses, net margin, debt ratio, growth rates and more. It will be good to compare the numbers and ratios across time. By analyzing these current and past data, it will allow you to evaluate the prospects of the company.

Balance Sheet

The company balance sheet provides an overview of the company's financial condition. The balance sheet consists of a section listing the company assets and another listing the liabilities and equity. The assets section is broken down into the company's cash and cash equivalents; investments; trade receivables or accounts receivables; inventories; deferred tax assets; intangible assets; goodwill; property, plant and equipment; and other assets. These might not be the same for every company though.

The liabilities section list the company's accounts payable, accrued liabilities, convertible notes, long term debt, other noncurrent liabilities, and any other outstanding debts that the company may have. The Shareholders' equity section reflects how much money is invested in the company in addition to cumulative retained earnings. Again, these might be different for other companies.

Income Statement

The company's income statement tells you how much the company is making and how much it has paid out over a year or in a quarter. It will be good to look at the annual income statement rather than the quarterly statement to give you a better idea of the company's overall position. Do remember that value investors are long-term investors so it is important that when you look at the income statement, you see long-term profitability.

Next, we will talk about Buffett's methodology.

Here we will look at how Buffett assesses and spots fair or undervalued stocks by asking a series of questions to evaluate the stock's quality and its relation to the price:

I.   Has the company performed well consistently?

Buffett looks at the Return on Equity (ROE) which is referred to as Stockholder's return on investment. It shows how much shareholders are earning income on their shares. By looking at the ROE, you can see if the company is performing well consistently as compared to other companies in the same industry. An investor should look at the ROE over the past 5 to 10 years for the historical performance.

ROE= Net Income / Shareholder's Equity

II.   Has the company avoided excess debt?

Buffett will consider the Debt/Equity Ratio. He loves to see a company taking as little debt as possible so that the earnings growth is being generated from shareholders' equity as opposed to borrowed money.

Debt/Equity Ratio = Total Liabilities / Shareholders' Equity

The Debt/Equity Ratio shows the proportion of equity and debt the company is using to finance its asset. The higher the ratio, it means more debt is used to finance the company. A high debt level compared to equity can result in volatile earnings and a large amount of interest expenses. The more stringent test is to use long-term debt to equity ratio.

III.   Are profit margins high? Are they increasing?

Buffett looks at a company's profitability, which means a good profit margin and whether the company is increasing it consistently. This margin is calculated by dividing the net income by the net sales. A good investor will consider at least 5 years of historical results. A high-profit margin suggests that the company is executing its business well. If the company is also increasing its margins, this means the management has been extremely efficient and successful at controlling expenses.

IV.   How long has the company been public?

Buffett tends to consider only companies which have been around for at least 10 years. As a result, most of the technology companies that had their initial public offerings (IPOs) in the past decade wouldn't get on the radar. It is important to select companies which have stood the test of time but are fair or undervalued.

You should never underestimate the value of historical performance which demonstrates a company's ability to increase shareholder value, though do note that a stock's past performance does not guarantee future performance. The job of the value investor is to determine how well the company can perform as it did in the past.

V.   Do the company's products rely on a commodity?

Buffett tends to shy away from companies whose products are non-differentiated from its competitors, and those that rely solely on a commodity such as oil and gas. If the company does not offer a different product or service from its competitor within the same industry, there is little to set the company apart and this will greatly reduce the company's economic moat or competitive advantage. Buffett loves a company with a huge economic moat in the form of a competitive advantage, e.g. brand loyalty, frequent daily usage, technology patent, etc. The wider the moat, the tougher it will be for the competitors to gain market share from the company.

VI. Is the stock selling at a 25 to 30% discount to its intrinsic value?

After you have identified the companies that can meet the above criteria, the next thing is to determine if the stocks are undervalued. This is considered the most difficult part of value investing. This is, in fact, Buffett's most prized skill. As a value investor, you must determine a company's intrinsic value by looking at a number of business fundamentals including earnings. One common way is to use the discounted cash flow model to assess the future value of the company.

Once Buffett determines the intrinsic value of the company, he compares it to its current market capitalization (current total worth). If the intrinsic value measurement is at least 25% higher than the company's market capitalization, Buffett sees the company as one that has value. Buffett's success is dependent on his unmatched skill in determining the intrinsic value. However, you can be as successful as him in which I will share in the later part.

The bottom-line

Buffett's investing style reflects a practical, down-to-earth attitude which is so simple yet inspiring. Buffett also maintains this attitude in other areas of his life: He doesn't live in an expensive house, he doesn't collect cars and he doesn't take a limousine to work. Whether you support Buffett or believe in his investing methods, the proof is in the pudding. He is valued at about US$85 billion as of 2019.

How to evaluate which stocks or market to enter?

I will share some enhanced and accelerated insights to help you evaluate which stocks or market to enter!

You can enter any market, though I tend to focus on the U.S. and Singapore markets as a personal choice. For the U.S. market, there is a strong and consistent growth over the decades. As for the Singapore market, I focus more on dividend stocks and REITs.

To adopt Buffett's way of evaluating stock using the value investing method, there will be two parts to it: Qualitative and Quantitative aspects of the fundamental analysis.

In the qualitative aspect, you will need to ask these few questions or perform this homework:

	Checklist
1	Is this stock within your circle of competence?
2	Do you understand what the business is doing?
3	How long has the company gone public (IPO)? The company should be listed on the stock exchange for at least 10years or more.
4	Is the company able to raise prices?
5	Do the company's products rely on a commodity? E.g. it will be good to avoid the company that relies too much on a commodity as it wouldn't be able to differentiate itself or can be overly reliant which may impact the company should that commodity be made unavailable.
6	Does the company have an economic moat or competitive advantage? E.g. A strong brand name, or has monopolized a certain market share, or have exclusive intellectual property rights.
7	Will the company still be in business over the next 5-10 years?
8	What type of company is it? (E.g. Growth, dividends, value).

In the quantitative aspect, you can refer to the table below for the selection criteria:

	Selection Criteria
1	Market Capitalization: more than $50 Billion
2	Debt to Equity Ratio: less than 1 or below 0.5
3	Long Term Debt to Equity Ratio: less than 1 or below 0.5
4	Return on Equity (ROE): more than 15%
5	Return on Investment (ROI): more than 15%
6	Earnings per share (EPS) growth last 5 years: positive
7	Earnings per share (EPS) growth next 5 years: positive
8	Profit margins %: more than 15%
9	Revenue growth % last 10 years: positive
10	Net income growth % last 10 years: positive
11	Profit growth % last 10 years: positive
12	Payout ratio: less than 50%. Is the earnings per share or free cash flow per share greater than the dividends per share?
13	Look at the ROE trend past 5 to 10 years: should be positive
14	Look at EPS trend past 5 to 10 years: should be positive
15	Look at Net Income trend past 5 to 10 years: should be positive

So far, this selection criteria list has served me well in terms of covering the fundamental analysis recommended by Buffett. Ultimately, you want to find a company that can deliver growing profits, earnings and revenue, has relatively low debt and can produce a high return on equity in a sustainable and consistent manner!

When is a good time to buy?

Firstly, don't follow the crowd. In Buffett's 2008 letter, he also said, "Beware the investment activity that produces applause; the great moves are usually greeted by yawns." In his 2009 letter, Buffett said to his investors, "It's been an ideal period for investors: a climate of fear is their best friend." Those who invest only when commentators are upbeat end up paying a heavy price for meaningless reassurance.

It's known that the average stock investor tends to underperform the market over time and it may be due to the investors buying and selling of investments too often and at the wrong time. When people see others selling, they tend to panic sell. When they see others making money from a rising market, they tend to invest all their money in. Instead of the common concept of "buy low, sell high", many investors tend to do the opposite.

One general rule is that timing the market will result in a losing battle but we will share some guidelines and metrics to help you decide when to buy stocks in the market. As Buffett says, "Widespread fear is your friend as an investor, because it serves up bargain purchases." One opportunity is when there is a market correction or a market crash; that's when true value investors will go smiling.

I will share some good value investing ratios which can help you to determine if the current price is fair, overvalued or undervalued when compared to the intrinsic value.

Price to Earnings P/E Ratio

The P/E ratio is called the earnings multiple; it means that the price of the stock is trading at X many times. This P/E ratio helps investors to determine the market value of a stock as compared to the company's earnings. The P/E ratio shows what the market is willing to pay today for a stock based on its past or future earnings. A high P/E ratio could mean that a stock's price is high relative to its earnings and could be possibly overvalued.

The average P/E for the S&P 500 has historically ranged from 13 to 15, and hence Buffett recommended looking at stocks which have a P/E ratio of 15 and below. The P/E ratio needs to be considered with similar companies within the same industry.

$$P/E \text{ ratio} = \text{stock price/ earnings per share}$$

PEG ratio

Given the P/E ratio is calculated using a forward earnings estimate, it does not always show whether the P/E ratio is appropriate for the company's forecasted growth rate. Hence, we will also be looking at the PEG ratio.

The PEG ratio will measure the relationship between the price/earnings ratio and the earnings growth to provide investors with a more complete story. This will allow investors to calculate whether a stock price is overvalued or undervalued in relation to the expected growth rate of the company in the future.

PEG ratios tend to vary across different sectors, but typically, a stock with PEG ratio of close to 1 or below is considered undervalued since the price is considered to be low compared to the company's expected earnings growth. A company with a PEG ratio of more than 1 is considered to be overvalued.

$$PEG\ ratio = P/E\ /\ EPS\ growth$$

Overall, you can buy the stock when the buy price is 25 to 30% below the intrinsic value or when the stock's PEG ratio is close to 1 or below.

In order to check the intrinsic value, you can go to *Gurufocus* website which is free. This is a very good website which provides you many valuable figures to evaluate the fundamentals of the company. Search for the company you're interested in, and then click on the section 'Discounted Cash Flow' (DCF).

The website will calculate for you the fair value and the current margin of safety based on the current stock price in comparison to the fair/intrinsic value. The parameters will be tabulated based on the past fundamental figures.

Assuming you have done your homework and identified the stocks properly on your waiting list, the next step is to wait for the price to fall within your selection criteria. This will take some patience. Sometimes, it may take a couple of years for the stock to reach the selection criteria or price target range; this is okay as long as you are confident in the stock's potential value!

When is it a good time to sell?

Imagine your stock has been losing its fundamental value or has been on a decline. This is when you start to wonder if you should sell the stock to offload the holdings, preserve the capital and hopefully be able to reinvest the funds into more profitable stocks. In the perfect world, you can achieve it by selling the stock at the right time; however it isn't that easy in real life. When the dotcom bubble burst in 2000 and the subprime mortgage crisis took place in 2008, many investors were frozen with fear. Many didn't react until their portfolio declined by 50 to 60%.

We will need a predetermined sell strategy to prevent excessive losses. By having a predetermined sell strategy, this allows us to have no emotional attachment and to act rationally as much as possible when it comes to whether or not the stock should be sold.

You may want to consider an adaptable selling strategy. This allows you to consider various factors in deciding when to sell.

If you are thinking about selling the stock, you need to ask yourself these questions:

- Why did you buy the stock in the first place (go back to the fundamentals)?
- What has changed about the company, if any?
- Does this change affect your initial reason for investing in that company?

As reflected in the first question, did you buy the company stock because it had solid financial statements? Was it developing the latest technology or patent and if so, was there any change to that, which gives rise to the second question?

Usually, when the stock price goes down, there can be multiple reasons for that. Does the quality that you originally liked in the company still exist? Has the attribute of the company changed fundamentally?

Assuming there has been a fundamental change, you will then need to answer the third question: is the change fundamental enough for you to decide not to buy the company based on the selection criteria? Remember not to get emotionally attached to companies and to make strategic decisions and smart sell positions when the need arises.

Using a value investor's approach to decide when to sell:

i.   You can choose to sell when the stock has reached its intrinsic value.

ii.   You can also sell the stock when the P/E ratio is nearing 40, which shows that stock could be highly overvalued.

iii. However, if the stock price were to fall by 20%, you should not sell immediately. Take some time to research on its fundamentals, e.g. refer to the list of selection criteria when buying a stock.

iv.   Supposed the company's ROE, EPS, revenue and net income start to decline over 2 years. If this is reflected in the stock price due to a fundamental change in the business, you can decide to sell the stock to minimize further loss.

v.   If the stock has a low P/E ratio but high earnings growth, you can still consider holding on to it or buy more of the stock as it is selling at a discount.

Overall, there is no hard and fast rule on what a value investor should follow, but still, it will be good to have an exit strategy which I shared earlier. This will greatly reduce the odds of the company stock being worthless, which is highly unlikely if we bought fundamentally strong stocks at the beginning, though there is no guarantee that a stock will continue to grow forever. The fundamental key attribute is to think critically about selling, stay disciplined with that strategy and keep your emotions out of the market.

About Growth Investing

Interestingly, growth investing and value investing have similar investing methodologies to some extent and there can be synergy. While both growth investor and value investor will expect to gain profit from price appreciation, growth investors will want to see a 5 year growth rate of 15% and above per year and expect the investment to potentially double in value. Plus, they may not be too bothered should the stock become overvalued as long as the price is rising and the growth is expected to keep up.

Like value investors, growth investors also do focus on earnings and profit growths, and they are crucial to driving the stock price appreciation at a higher rate. Do note that a growth stock can actually be a value stock if it is priced appropriately and has sound fundamentals.

These are some key questions to ask:

i.   Does the company have any identifiable consumer monopolies or brand name?

ii.   Do you understand how the business works?

iii.   Is the company conservatively financed in terms of having a long term debt to equity ratio of less than 0.5?

iv.   Are the earnings (e.g. EPS) of the company strong and do they show an upward trend?

v.   Does the company allocate capital only to businesses within its realm of expertise/circle of competence?

vi.   Does the company consistently earn a high rate of return on shareholders' equity?

vii.   Does the company get to retain its earnings?

viii.   How much does the company have to spend on maintaining current operations?

ix.   Is the company free to reinvest its retained earnings in new business opportunities?

x.   Is the company free to adjust prices to inflation?

xi.   Will the value-addedness of retained earnings increase the market value of the company?

Chapter 15

Value Investing Options Strategy

Now that we have already shared with you about index investing, dividend investing and even value investing which is already the pinnacle of Buffett's investing strategy, how else can you make your stocks work even harder?

Did you know that Warren Buffett uses the option strategy? In this chapter, we will take a look at how it actually complements the value investing strategy.

What are Options?

Options are defined as conditional derivative contracts which allow buyers or sellers of the contracts to buy or sell a stock at a chosen price.

Option buyers are charged an amount called a "premium" by the option sellers for allowing them to enjoy the right. Should the market prices turn unfavorable, be they go up or down, the option buyers can choose to exercise the options. Generally, option sellers will assume greater risk than option buyers, hence they will demand the "premium" which we will explain more in detail about the strategy.

Options can be classified into Call and Put options.

- Buy a Call option: the buyer purchases the right to buy the underlying asset, e.g. stocks in the future at a predetermined price called the exercise price or strike price.

- Sell a Call option: the seller sells the right to the buyer to buy the underlying asset, e.g. stocks in future at the strike price (the seller gets to sell the stock).
- Buy a Put option: the buyer purchases the right to sell the underlying asset, e.g. stocks in future at the strike price.
- Sell a Put option: the seller sells the right to the buyer to sell the underlying asset, e.g. stocks in future at the strike price (the seller gets to buy the stock).

Other key contract terms will include the contract size, which for stocks, is usually in denominations of 100 shares per contract. The expiration date specifies when the option expires or matures. American options let an investor exercise an option any time before the expiration date.

Does Warren Buffett do option investing?

Wait a minute, didn't Warren Buffett use to publicly criticize derivatives being financial instruments of mass destruction, so why are we talking about options here?

Did you know that Buffett has been selling long term Put options on many publicly traded indexes? In Berkshire's 2008 letter to the shareholders, Buffett discusses options and the Black-Scholes model (widely used a mathematical model for valuing options). Let's dive in to see what Buffett has to say about option strategy!

Buffett explains that his strategy is on two levels. First, he sells overvalued options by writing puts with long horizons of more than 15 years, which are systematically overpriced. Second, he uses the premiums gained from selling the options to invest. The options Buffett has written are European, which means they can only be exercised at the expiration date and he doesn't need to worry about having to pay the value before expiration.

Buffett mentioned in his letter: "Our Put contracts total USD$37.1 billion (at current exchange rates) and are spread among four major indexes: the S&P500 in the U.S., the FTSE100 in the UK, the Euro Stoxx 50 in Europe, and the Nikkei 225 in Japan. Our first contract comes due on Sep 9, 2019, and our last on Jan 24, 2028. We have received premiums of US$4.9 billion, the money we have invested."

Wow, can you imagine that? Buffett has been selling Put options and enjoying additional premiums or returns on his stocks.

Buffett also went on to explain why he sells a long-term Put option on indexes. By using the Black Scholes model, he uses a scenario and expected return format, anticipating a 99% chance that the value of the S&P 500 would rise over 100 years, a 1% chance that it would fall. He expects a loss of 50% of the index if it does fall. This shows Buffett uses fundamental estimated values to check the pricing of options, in line with the value investing approach.

But hold on.

We are not Warren Buffett so we can't write 15 to 20 year Put options like Buffett. However, we can still invest using the options strategy...

As retail investors, we are happy to know that there is plenty of liquidity in the options market for us to write Put options on individual companies, and these options can generate much higher premiums than options written on indexes.

The higher premiums are a result of the company-specific risk which are unlike indexes. The share price can go to zero, however, the individual options market is more mispriced relative to the long-run company fundamentals and this presents opportunities in the market. Though we can't write 15 years options, we can stick to selling long-term options where the company's fundamentals become more important. The strategy will be to sell options on fundamentally strong companies using the value investing approach. The idea is that we want stocks which will rise over time and hence we are willing to capture some of the time-horizon premiums from selling option.

Indeed, options may seem overwhelming but I will try to explain them to make it easier to understand. Selling options, on top of valued stocks, can enhance the investment portfolio. This advanced strategy allows added income and protection depending on the situation. One example is to use options as an effective hedge against a declining stock market to limit downside losses, e.g. selling a covered call option. Options are also an alternative to generate recurring income using Buffett's methodology.

When to sell Call Options versus Put Options?
By selling options, we are tapping into a very huge opportunity to turn time value decay (the reduction in the value of an option contract as it reaches its expiration date) into potential profits.

For example, when option sellers sell an option or establish a position, they collect time-value premiums paid by option buyers. As time passes, time-value decay becomes money and allows the option seller to benefit from the passage of time.

There are two main options strategies which are to sell a covered Call option or a protective Put option. With these 2 option strategies, it requires you to either first buy the stocks or be ready to buy the stocks with the required funds. There is no use of leverage margin accounts, in line with Buffett's take on minimizing debt and the use of leverage given that they are very dangerous should the market play against your favor.

For a covered Call option, this is the preferred method when you:

- already owned the stocks
- expect no change or a slight increase in the stock's price or feel bearish about the stock
- are willing to limit upside potential in exchange for some downside protection
- can limit profit potential if the underlying stock price rises sharply
- expect to maximize profit on the call option which is the premium received

A covered Call option strategy will involve you buying 100 shares of the stock and then selling a Call option contract at a strike price, expiring one month later, on those shares.

E.g. Suppose you buy 100 shares of stock X atUS$50 per share and then sell 1 Call option (1 option contract equals to 100 shares), with the strike price of US$52 expiring in one month. The premium will be US$0.3 per share, making it US$30 for 1 Call option contract. Immediately, you will be able to pocket US$30 premium. The US$0.3 premium per share reduces the cost basis on the shares to US$49.70. Any decline in the stock price to this point of US$49.70 will be offset by the premiums received from the option position, which offers limited downside protection.

If the share price goes above US$52 before expiration, the call option can be exercised, meaning the option seller has to sell the stock at the strike price. You will make a profit of US$2.30 per share (US$52 strike price minus US$49.70 cost basis).

If the stock does not rise above US$52 or drops before the expiration date, the option expires and becomes worthless, i.e. you still get to keep the stocks and can continue to repeat the strategy to write and sell another covered Call option.

When you sell Call options, you are betting that the stock price will remain below the strike price during the term of the option. As long as this happens, you can earn income from the strategy.

Till this point, this is just part of the equation. I will touch on selling protective Put options next. If you wish to own value stocks at a discount, you can sell more protective Put options. I will share how selling both covered call and protective options can complement each other.

For Protective Put options, this is the preferred method when you:

- want to own the stock
- feel bullish about the stock

A protective Put option strategy will involve you being prepared to buy 100 shares of the stock with the funds ready and then selling a Put option contract at a strike price, expiring one month later, on those shares.

If the price of the stock increases and goes above the put's strike price near the expiration date, the option becomes worthless. However, if the stock price decreases to the put's strike price, then the option seller is able to buy the stocks at a discounted price.

E.g. Suppose you potentially want to buy 100 shares of stock X at US$50 per share (identified through value investing approach and this is a fundamentally strong stock) and then sell 1 protective call option (1 option contract equals to 100 shares), with the strike price of US$48 expiring in one month. The premium will be US$0.3 per share, making it US$30 for 1 option contract. Immediately, you will be able to pocket US$30 premium.

If the stock price stays above the US$48 strike price, you will get the premiums given as the put option approaches the expiration date one month later, the time-value will decay and make the put option worthless. The maximum profit on the put option will be US$30 collected.

However, if the stock price moves below the US$48 strike price, the Put option will be exercised and you will be able to purchase the stock at US$48, which is below the initial market price of US$50. The theoretical risk for selling Put option is that the option seller will still have to buy the stock at US$48 even if the stock price falls to zero. With the value investing approach to identify fundamentally strong stocks, we aim to minimize the risk of the stock falling to zero, though there is still a possibility.

When you sell put options, you are taking the view that the stock price will remain above the strike price during the term of the option. As long as this happens, you can earn income from this protective Put options strategy with the premiums.

If you look at this method, it is potentially a win-win situation. If the Put option is not exercised, you would have earned the premiums. If the Put option is exercised, you get to buy the stocks, which you already have the intentions to do so, at a lower price.

How to set the strike price for Call and Put options?

When it comes to setting the strike price for options, it can be any of the followings:

- In the money option
- Out of the money option
- At the money option

	Put Option	Call Option
In the money option	The strike price of the option is greater than the price of the stock.	The strike price of the option is less than the price of the stock.
Out of the money option	**The strike price of the option is less than the price of the stock.**	**The strike price of the option is greater than the price of the stock.**
At the money option	The strike price of the option is equal to the price of the stock.	The strike price of the option is equal to the price of the stock.

The idea is to sell covered Call options or protective Put options to be out of the money. For a Call option, out of the money option means the strike price is set higher than the current stock price in the market. A Put option, out of the money option means the strike price is set lower than the current stock price in the market.

The value of the put option decreases due to time decay because of the probability of the stock falling below the strike price decreases. This is in line with the belief that fundamentally strong stocks will appreciate over time. The thing is that we want the option to lose its time value and when the expiration date is reached, we want the option to have zero intrinsic value, e.g. out of the money option and at the money options. This means the options buyers will not want to exercise the option.

- Put options become less valuable or lose its value when the stock price increases.
- Call options become less valuable or lose its value when the stock price decreases.

To use this options strategy to earn additional "premium" income every month, we want to set out of the money options so that as the option reaches the expiration date, it will become worthless and expires. This will free up the cash flow for us to repeat the strategy many times.

The volatility of the option

Based on the example of Wells Fargo, the option premiums tend to be lower as the stock is quite stable and not so volatile. If you look at the Bid column, it shows the premium to be

US$0.76 for the strike price of US$48 and the premium return is about 1.58%. Ideally, we should aim for a premium return of 2% and above.

Volatility will increase the price of the option. Due to uncertainty which may push the odds of an outcome higher, option buyers are willing to pay more to protect the downside. If the volatility of the stock increases, the price swings will increase the possibilities of large price movements, resulting in higher chances of an event occurring. Hence, the greater the volatility of the stock, the higher the premium of the option will be.

Please take note that when considering higher premium returns of the options sold, you may also be exposing yourself to more risk exposure, volatility and sudden price movements in that particular stock.

Chapter 16

Brokerage Account

In this chapter, you will learn how to select a brokerage account and how to execute the buying strategy to minimize the transaction fees.

Stock brokerage accounts will provide you access to stock exchanges so that you can buy and sell stocks and other listed securities. Some brokerage will only provide access to one particular stock market while some provide access to most major global stock exchanges.

When deciding the stock brokerage to choose, always remember the lesson learned in Chapter 12 on index investing, which is to keep your expense ratio or brokerage fees as low as possible.

When we compare stock brokerage accounts, one major factor to consider is the commission fees they charge.

    a.   Brokerage Fees

The brokerage fee is charged by the platform provider to conduct transactions between buyers and sellers. Usually, the brokerage will charge a percentage of the transaction amount or a minimum fee, whichever is higher.

    b.   Central Depository Account versus Custodian

In Singapore, the Central Depository Account (CDP) is a securities account to hold all your stocks. Stocks can be bought from various brokerage firms but all the stocks will be stored in one CDP account, e.g. POEMs, Kim Eng, DBS Vickers, etc.

However, some investors are comfortable to have their stocks held in a bank acting as a custodian, e.g. Standard Chartered or even some of the U.S. brokerage such as TD Ameritrade, Interactive Brokers, etc.

- Brokerage accounts that hold your shares as a custodian tend to be the cheapest. However, please note that should the bank or custodian collapses, your stocks will go down the drain as well (some brokerage accounts do have an insured sum up to a certain amount).
- Holding the stocks in the CDP ensures a higher security though the fees tend to be higher.

For those investing in the U.S. market, you can consider TD Ameritrade or Interactive Brokers as their commission fees are extremely attractive for U.S. stocks.

In2019, Best Online Brokers Awards, Interactive Brokers received awards for Best Overall Online Brokers, Best for Low Costs, Best for Options Trading, Best for Penny Stocks, Best for Day Trading, and Best for International Trading.

TD Ameritrade has the following accolades under its belt: Best Overall Online Brokers, Best for Beginners, Best Stock Trading Apps, Best for ETFs, Best for Options Trading, Best for Roth IRAs, Best for IRAs, Best for Day Trading and, Best Web Trading Platforms.

For the Singapore market or London stock exchange (in case you plan on getting index ETF domiciled in Ireland), you can consider Standard Chartered.

Brokerage Companies (in Singapore)	Minimum Brokerage Fees	Trading Fees (based on contract amount)		
		(S$)		
		<$50K	$50K to $100K	>$100K
KGI Securities	$25	0.28%	0.22%	0.18%
CGS-CIMB Securities	$25	0.28%	0.22%	0.18%
DBS Vickers	$25	0.28%	0.22%	0.18%
Maybank Kim Eng	$25	0.28%	0.22%	0.18%
Lim & Tan Securities	$25	0.28%	0.22%	0.18%
Phillips Securities (POEMS)	$25	0.28%	0.22%	0.18%
OCBC Securities	$25	0.28%	0.22%	0.18%
UOB KayHian	$25	0.28%	0.22%	0.20%
RHB Securities	$25	0.28%	0.22%	0.18%
FSMOne.com	$10	0.08%	0.08%	0.08%
Citibank	$28	0.25%	0.20%	0.18%
Standard Chartered	$10	0.20%	0.20%	0.20%
Saxo Capital Markets	$9-$15	0.10% to 0.12%	0.10% to 0.12%	0.10% to 0.12%

If need be, I suggest setting up two brokerage accounts separately for U.S. stocks and Singapore stocks to enjoy the best of both worlds.

Generally speaking, for any actively managed account, the transaction fees should be below 1%. For an index/ETF investing, the transaction fees should be below 0.3%. Many Vanguard and Schwab index funds charge much less than this so this can be a good benchmark.

How often to buy – Lump sum versus Dollar Cost Averaging (DCA)?

This is a common question and you can learn how to schedule your investment.

Dollar Cost Averaging (DCA) is a method whereby the investor sets a fixed amount to invest at regular intervals. DCA is a good strategy for investors with lower risk tolerance and for those who do not want to time the market. By doing DCA, you are also able to spread out the investment cost as you will be buying into the market during the ups and downs. Another good time to use DCA is when the market is about to crash or on a decline. You can purchase large portions or number of the shares in a declining market.

For lump sum investing, it will lean slightly more towards the timing of the market or when the stock is within fair or under-value range. You may also run the risk of buying at the peak though with the proper value investing approach, you should know how to manage the risk before entering into the market. The plus side is that because you enter a lump sum at the right time, there is more upside potential for your overall sum to work harder and compound versus spreading via DCA. If you are willing to be an active investor, you may make more returns on investment using Buffett's methodologies which I have covered in the earlier chapters.

Be it DCA or lump sum investing, one recommendation is to accumulate at least $10,000 before making any buy. This is to significantly reduce the brokerage fee ratio to less than 1% of your invested amount.

Chapter 17

How To Do Portfolio Management

We have kept the best for the last and this is one of the most important segments and competencies on how to manage your portfolio in a sustainable manner.

Portfolio investment is somewhat like a science and art of building a combination of assets to achieve the required rate of return over a period of time. It entails buying and selling of securities such as stocks, bonds, ETFs, REITs, real estate, etc. Essentially, it is about asset allocation, risk diversification and management, and portfolio balancing.

Factors affecting the portfolio investment:

- Age: it defines your financial priorities and goals.
- Risk tolerance: it determines if and how much you can invest in risk assets.
- Time Horizon: this aspect is related to fulfilling specific financial goals and how much time is left to fulfill them.

Key Elements of Portfolio Management

a. Asset Allocation

One of the keys to portfolio management is about the mix of the asset. Asset allocation is about understanding the different types of assets, e.g. stocks, bonds, cash, etc. Asset allocation is about trying to optimize the risk and returns profile of an investor. For example, investors with a more aggressive profile can lean their portfolio towards more volatile investments. Investors with a more conservative profile can balance their portfolio towards less volatile investments.

b. Diversification

Generally, it is a prudent approach to have a basket of investment that provides broad exposure within an asset class. Diversification is like spreading the risk and returns within the asset class as it may be sometimes difficult to know which investment can outperform another. Diversification is usually recommended to be across different asset class, sectors of the economy and geographical regions.

c. Rebalancing

Rebalancing is key to helping an investor return the portfolio to the targeted asset/portfolio mix allocation. This is crucial to ensure that the portfolio best reflects the investor's risk and return profile especially as one ages and experiences changing life priorities. Sometimes, the movement of the stock markets could alter and expose the portfolio to greater risk. Rebalancing may also take place amongst allocating the fund percentage within the particular asset class.

Understanding your risk appetite?

After understanding the factors and elements of portfolio management, the next step is to understand your level of risk appetite. In terms of time horizon, it is recommended that you invest for the long run with the Buffett investing methodology.

It is key to understand your risk appetite and tolerance as this can help determine your preferred investing strategy.

When it comes to risk appetite or tolerance, you will have to first assess your personal take and comfort level with the historical worst-case scenarios and returns for the various asset classes. Are you prepared to lose money or experience paper loss during the bad years, e.g. market crashes? Typically, the risk appetite spectrum can range from being aggressive, moderate to conservative.

- Aggressive Risk Appetite

Aggressive investors tend to be more market and investment savvy. They do understand more on securities, risk, and returns and can work them to their advantage while being able to withstand the volatile market fluctuations. Aggressive investors tend to go for high returns accompanied by high risk.

- Moderate Risk Appetite

Moderate investors tend to be able to accept some risk but aim to adopt a more balanced approach with an intermediate time horizon of 5 to 10 years. The moderate investors' portfolio might have some equities coupled with bonds and cash, split around 60-40 or 50-50. Some moderate investors might also split the portfolio 50-50 when it comes to investing in dividend stocks/REITs and value stocks.

- Conservative Risk Appetite

Conservative investors tend to accept little to no volatility within their investment portfolio. Typically, they are usually retirees or people nearing retirement. They have spent years to accumulate their investment/retirement funds and prefer to protect their principal as much as possible. The conservative investor also tends to prefer more guaranteed and liquidity investment options. For example, it can be bonds, cash or low-risk investment just to beat inflation or allow preservation of the fund.

This table summarizes the returns, risk appetite and liquidity preferences for investors across different age range.

Age Range	Goals	Return Expectations	Risk Appetite	Liquidity
20-30 years old	Education, Marriage, Holiday	High	High	Low
30-40 years old	Children, Education, Insurance	Moderately High	Moderately High	Moderately Low
40-50 years old	Children's Marriage, Retirement	Balanced	Balanced	Balanced
50-60 years old	Retirement	Moderately Low	Moderately Low	Moderately High
Above 60 years old	Holidays, Estate Planning	Low	Low	High

All investments will carry varying degree of risk. In order to make an informed decision, you will need to identify possible and potential risks and see if you are willing to accept them. Your risk tolerance will change as your investment goals, financial situation, and life experience change. Generally, the longer the time horizon you can allow your money to be invested, the more risk you can afford to take. Of course, you should still invest with your circle of competence and apply the Buffett investing methodology.

How to manage the risk?

One of the ways to manage the risk is to have diversification in the portfolio. By investing in a range of assets, you will reduce the risk of one investment or stock's performance severely lowering the return of your overall investment. It is true that you shouldn't put all of your eggs into one basket; even Buffett himself invests in various stocks to diversify across industry sectors.

When you start off with a small amount, e.g. US$1,000 or US$10,000, you may only be able to invest in one or two companies. Slowly as you start to acquire more stocks, you can redistribute the portfolio split to reduce the concentration into any particular stock and to spread the risk across in general.

For those who prefer the passive investing method, then you can invest in a well-diversified investment using the market or sector ETFs. The ETFs tend to have a large number of stocks or investments within the fund itself, which makes them more diversified compared to a single stock.

Types of portfolio investment

After understanding about risk and diversification, these are various types of portfolio investment which you can consider.

- Aggressive Portfolio

The aggressive portfolio tends to include stocks with high risk and high returns (provided you use the Buffett methodology). Stocks with higher risk also tend to have higher beta or sensitivity to the market. This means that high beta stocks can experience larger price fluctuations as well.

Companies with aggressive stock offerings tend to be in the growth stage. Investors wanting an aggressive portfolio usually go for growth stocks or companies with rapidly accelerating earnings growth. Most of the time, these companies are technology-related as many firms in the technology industry tend to pursue an aggressive growth strategy. Risk management will be highly important for someone with an aggressive portfolio. The investor needs to be very competent and knows the market and investing strategies very well, including having an exit strategy.

- Defensive Portfolio

For investors who want a defensive portfolio, they usually choose those stocks with a lower beta. For example, stocks or companies that make and sell basic necessities (a favorite category of Buffett) tend to do better even during recessionary times. No matter how bad the economy is, people will still buy basic necessities which are essential for daily living. This allows companies to make money even in those times. An example will be consumer staples, etc.

A key advantage of buying cyclical stocks is that they offer an extra level of protection, but we will also need to evaluate those stocks against our Buffett selection criteria checklist. Given that these stocks are often in demand, the stock prices may be overvalued, so please do check the valuation first! For starting investors, it may be prudent to include more defensive stocks in the portfolio as well.

- Income Portfolio

This investor will focus more on earning money through dividends back to shareholders. The stock companies are usually safe and defensive while giving out dividends. With an income portfolio, this investing strategy should generate positive cash flow. REITs are another good example to include as part of the income portfolio mix. REITs tend to give back most of the profits given the favorable tax status.

Having an income portfolio can be a good complement to the investor's portfolio to support one's retirement fund. Investors may keep a lookout for undervalued stocks or REITs that can still maintain a reasonably high dividend yield backed by strong fundamentals. Often, these types of companies or stocks can supplement income and also allow investors to enjoy capital gains over time.

How to determine the portfolio mix using a rule of thumb?

Next, looking at your whole investment portfolio, do you know how much to split between stocks or cash or bonds, etc.?

Given that the average life expectancy is about 85 years, we can use this formula: which is to take 110 years minus your current age. This is the percentage you should allocate for stocks.

(110 – Your Age) = % of the investment portfolio that should be allocated in equities

For example, you are 30 years old, it will be 110 minus 30 equals to 80. Your investment portfolio can roughly make up of 80% stocks, with 20% in cash and bonds or other low risk and high liquidity investment options.

As you approach your retirement age, you should shift your investment portfolio towards low-risk investment options. One suggestion is to do a major re-balancing when you reach your decade milestone, e.g. 30 years old, 40 years old, 50 years old. Alternatively, you can do it every year to nail your portfolio down to the percentage point.

How to determine the percentage split for the stocks and number of stocks in the portfolio?

Based on past research papers, an investor should hold about 20 to 30 stocks in his / her portfolio. However, I would suggest holding about up to 10 stocks first. Should you wish to include the option strategy, then you may go up to 20 stocks. It doesn't mean the more stocks you have, the better it will be. Remember what Buffett taught about having too much diversification which arises when you do not have the competence.

If you have up to 10 stocks or counters, you have effectively allocated your funds to be about 10% to 20% per stock. Always remember not to put all of your eggs into one basket and to only invest in your own circle of competence.

If you are doing passive investing through market index ETFs, you are actually required to hold even fewer counters because the index ETFs would have covered a wide range of stocks for diversification.

How to review and rebalance your portfolio easily?

It is good to review your investment from time to time so that you can tell if your allocations are out of balance. A typical moderate portfolio for value and income strategy will be about 60% stocks and 40% bonds. An aggressive portfolio, which is for people with higher risk tolerance and a longer time horizon of 10 years and more, can hold about 80% stocks and 20% bonds.

Step 1

You can visit the free Instant X-Ray tool at *www.morningstar.com*. You can input your fund and stock symbols in the first column and put the dollar value of each stock holding in the second column.

Step 2

This shows a breakdown of your portfolio. The "X-Ray" will show how much you have in stocks, bonds, cash, as well as how the assets and holdings are divided by the sectors, e.g. finance, technology, etc. It will also list all the stocks you hold, including the ones in the funds you own, ranked by weight.

Step 3

After seeing the X-Ray's result of your portfolio breakdown, you need to assess if there are any potential weaknesses. Is your current portfolio skewed towards one particular sector or asset class?

The tool will also show and compare your annual fees to a similarly weighted model portfolio. If you ended up paying much more in annual fees, you might be better off looking for comparable lower cost index ETFs.

How does Buffett manage his portfolio?

Finally, the finale! You must be wondering how Warren Buffett manages his portfolio.

Let's go back to when Buffett first started out as an investor back in 1956 when he launched his partnership. Buffett's portfolio was much smaller, and this allowed him to go after the greatest inefficiencies he was able to find in the market. One key focus for Buffett was to find stocks selling at a cheap or fair valuation.

Buffett was even not afraid to invest up to 25% of his portfolio into one stock or company. He even stated that he would be comfortable investing up to 40% of his network into one single security if the probabilities were assessed to be extremely in his favor. Of course, we are not like Buffett, so please do not go and invest 40% of your net-worth into one stock unless it is an index ETF.

Today, Warren Buffett's portfolio remains more concentrated. Did you know that his four largest positions each account for over 10% of Berkshire Hathaway's portfolio? He believes in running a concentrated portfolio, given a few excellent businesses and investment opportunities made available at a given time. Owning too many positions reduces the impact of the best investment selections.

Also, Buffett's investment strategy has always been centered on the concept of staying within one's circle of competence. In his own words, "Risk comes from not knowing what you are doing." In other words, you should not invest in a business or industry if the model is hard to understand. In fact, the reality is that most investment opportunities may fall outside of our circle of competence and should be ignored – so stay focus!

Right from the days of Buffett's initial partnership, his investment strategy has evolved to concentrating more on owning wonderful businesses at reasonable prices rather than diving for cheap stocks which might be of a lower quality. He will look for companies that have strong economic moats and have numerous opportunities for growth!

Chapter 18

Achieving F.I.R.E The Buffett Way / Afterword

Wow, you have made it to the end of the book. I hope this book has helped you to understand your WHY, retirement goals as well as end objectives. Also, I hope this book has provided you with a range of investment strategies which you can adopt accordingly depending on your objective, time horizon, and risk appetite as an investor.

Identifying and understanding your WHY will be important as it will help and motivate you to achieve your F.I.R.E. What will be that meaningful purpose of your life? How will F.I.R.E help you pursue your life mission?

Money in itself is not the end but only a mean. By discovering the Buffett way of investing, you can create and grow your wealth in a sustainable manner, just like how Buffett found deep learning in Benjamin Graham's investing philosophy. By learning a range of investing strategies and methodologies, you can wait for that perfect pitch in the investment game, just like how Buffett will strike with his business perspective investing bat when the business and price is right.

The reality is many will have difficulty waiting patiently for that right moment and may end up investing less efficiently. By learning the various strategies and selection criteria, you can learn the subtleties of each strategy to choose one which will suit you the best. In addition, you will now know how to distinguish real investment opportunities from those that invite folly and be a contrarian investor just like Buffett.

Always remember to be "fearful when others are greedy and greedy when others are fearful." Pessimism will present the most valuable opportunity.

Going to the very beginning, I wish for this book to give you the financial freedom and time together with the investing competence to grow your happiness. Through achieving your F.I.R.E, it can also help you gain back time with your family and loved ones, and open new opportunities to pursue your meaning and aspiration in life. Remember, the most important investment you can make is in yourself!

I'm sure we can all achieve our F.I.R.E the Buffett way!

God bless,

Benjamin

www.ingramcontent.com/pod-product-compliance
Lightning Source LLC
Chambersburg PA
CBHW030802180526
45163CB00003B/1133